BEST FOOD
COLLECTION

figs with prosciutto

PREPARATION TIME

1 Arrange figs on serving platter, top with prosciutto. Drizzle figs with vinegar and sprinkle with pepper.

6 large black figs (500g), halved
6 thin slices prosciutto, halved
3 teaspoons balsamic vinegar

serves 6
per fig 1.4g fat; 253kJ (61 cal)
Recipe is best made just before serving.

spicy chicken salad in witlof

PREPARATION TIME   **COOKING TIME**

1 tablespoon sesame oil

300g chicken mince

1 tablespoon fish sauce

2 tablespoons lime juice

1 tablespoon palm sugar

1 tablespoon finely chopped
fresh vietnamese mint

1 tablespoon finely chopped
fresh coriander

4 baby witlof, separated

CORIANDER PASTE

2 coriander roots,
chopped coarsely

3 cloves garlic, peeled

4cm piece fresh ginger (20g),
grated finely

10 white peppercorns

1 Make coriander paste.

2 Heat oil in wok or large frying pan, add coriander paste; cook, stirring, until fragrant.

3 Add chicken, cook, stirring, until browned lightly.

4 Add sauce, juice and sugar to wok; simmer gently, uncovered, for a few minutes or until thickened slightly. Stir in mint and coriander.

5 Divide mixture evenly among witlof leaves.

CORIANDER PASTE In a small blender, spice grinder or mortar and pestle, blend or pound ingredients until finely chopped.

makes 24

per leaf 1.8g fat; 134kJ (32 cal)

TIPS The chicken filling can be prepared several hours ahead; keep covered in refrigerator. Assemble just before serving.

duck in crisp wonton cups

PREPARATION TIME   **COOKING TIME**

24 wonton wrappers

cooking-oil spray

1 chinese barbecued duck

1 tablespoon hoisin sauce

1 tablespoon soy sauce

2 tablespoons coarsely chopped
   fresh coriander

2 green onions, chopped coarsely

2 green onions, extra, sliced thinly

1 Preheat oven to moderate. Grease two 12-hole mini-muffin pans.
2 Press wonton wrappers into muffin pans to form a cup shape; spray
   lightly with oil. Bake in moderate oven about 8 minutes or until browned
   lightly. Remove from muffin pans, cool.
3 Remove flesh and skin from duck, slice thinly, discard fat. Place duck on
   oven tray, cover with foil; heat in moderate oven about 10 minutes.
4 Combine duck with sauces, coriander and chopped green onion in
   medium bowl; mix well.
5 Spoon duck mixture into wonton cases, top with extra green onion.

makes 24
per cup 8.5g fat; 496kJ (118 cal)
TIPS Wonton cases can be made a day ahead; store in an airtight
container. The filling can be prepared several hours ahead. Assemble
close to serving.

tandoori chicken on cucumber

PREPARATION TIME   **COOKING TIME**

1   Combine yogurt, tandoori paste and chicken in medium bowl.
    Refrigerate 30 minutes.
2   Cook chicken on hot grill plate or frying pan until cooked through.
    Cool slightly.
3   Slice cucumber into 1.5cm rounds, about eight rounds per cucumber.
    Using a teaspoon, scoop a small amount of the seeds from the centre
    of rounds, without scooping all the way through.
4   Slice chicken thinly, divide slices among cucumber rounds; top with
    the mint yogurt and coriander leaves.
    MINT YOGURT Combine ingredients in small bowl.

    makes 24
    per cucumber round 1g fat; 90kJ (22 cal)
    TIPS Chicken and yogurt can be prepared several hours ahead.
    Assemble close to serving.

2 tablespoons thick yogurt
2 tablespoons tandoori paste
200g chicken tenderloins
3 lebanese cucumbers (400g)
coriander leaves

MINT YOGURT

¼ cup (70g) thick yogurt
2 teaspoons finely shredded
    fresh mint
½ teaspoon ground coriander
½ teaspoon lime juice

little chicken and leek pies

PREPARATION TIME ~~~~~~~~~~~~~~ **COOKING TIME** ~~~~~~~~~~~~~~~~~~~~~~~~~

¾ cup (180ml) chicken stock

½ cup (125ml) dry white wine

2 single chicken breast fillets (340g)

20g butter

1 medium leek (350g),
  chopped finely

1 trimmed celery stalk (100g),
  chopped finely

1 tablespoon plain flour

2 teaspoons fresh
  lemon thyme leaves

½ cup (125ml) cream

1 teaspoon dijon mustard

4 sheets ready rolled
  shortcrust pastry

3 sheets ready rolled puff pastry

1 egg yolk, beaten lightly

lemon thyme leaves, extra

1 Combine stock and wine in medium saucepan; bring to a boil. Add chicken, return to a boil, cover; reduce heat, simmer about 10 minutes or until chicken is just cooked through. Remove from heat, stand chicken 10 minutes; remove chicken, reserve ¾ cup (180ml) cooking liquid; chop chicken finely.

2 Melt butter in medium saucepan; cook leek and celery, stirring, until soft. Add flour and thyme, stir until bubbling. Gradually stir in reserved liquid and cream; cook, stirring, until mixture boils and thickens. Stir in chicken and mustard. Remove from heat, cool slightly.

3 Preheat oven to hot. Grease three 12-hole patty pans.

4 Using 7cm cutter, cut 36 rounds from shortcrust pastry. Press into prepared pans. Spoon 1 tablespoon of chicken mixture into each pastry case. Using 6cm cutter, cut 36 rounds from puff pastry. Top chicken mixture with pastry lids, brush with egg yolk and sprinkle with extra thyme leaves.

5 Bake in hot oven about 15 minutes or until browned.

makes 36

per pie 10.5g fat; 711kJ (170 cal)

TIP Chicken mixture can be made a day ahead.

mussels with garlic crumbs

PREPARATION TIME   **COOKING TIME**

1 cup (70g) stale breadcrumbs
2 cloves garlic, chopped finely
1 teaspoon finely grated lemon rind
2 tablespoons finely chopped fresh
   flat-leaf parsley
1kg small black mussels
1½ cups (375ml) water
¼ cup (60ml) extra virgin olive oil

1 Combine breadcrumbs, garlic, rind and parsley in small bowl.
2 Wash and scrub mussels, remove fibrous beards by pulling firmly.
3 Bring the water to a boil in large saucepan; add mussels and boil, covered, about 7 minutes or until the mussels open, shaking pan occasionally. Discard any unopened mussels.
4 Break open shells, discard tops. Loosen mussels from shells with a spoon, replace in shells. Place shells, in single layer, on large baking tray.
5 Sprinkle mussels with breadcrumb mixture; drizzle with oil. Place under hot grill about 3 minutes or until browned.
6 Serve mussels immediately.

serves 8
per serving 7.6g fat; 473kJ (112 cal)
TIP The mussels can be prepared with the breadcrumb topping several hours ahead. Grill just before serving.

oysters with two dressings

PREPARATION TIME

SPICY LIME DRESSING

1½ tablespoons fresh lime juice
½ teaspoon peri peri sauce
1 teaspoon chopped
    fresh coriander
12 fresh oysters in half shell

Combine lime juice, sauce
and coriander in small bowl.
Spoon mixture over oysters.

makes 12
per oyster 0.2g fat; 34kJ (8 cal)

RED WINE VINEGAR DRESSING

1½ teaspoons finely
    chopped shallots
1 tablespoon red wine vinegar
1 teaspoon extra virgin olive oil
12 fresh oysters in half shell

Combine shallot, vinegar, oil,
and pepper in small bowl.
Spoon mixture over oysters.

makes 12
per oyster 0.6g fat; 46kJ (11 cal)

vegetable rice paper rolls
with chilli dipping sauce

PREPARATION TIME [35 MINUTES (PLUS STANDING TIME)] **COOKING TIME** [5 MINUTES (PLUS COOLING TIME)]

50g vermicelli noodles

2 medium avocados (500g)

1 medium carrot (120g)

100g garlic chives

24 small round rice paper wrappers

3 red radishes (100g),
　　grated coarsely

1 cup (80g) bean sprouts, trimmed

24 large mint leaves

CHILLI DIPPING SAUCE

½ cup (125ml) white vinegar

1 cup (220g) caster sugar

1 teaspoon salt

¼ cup (60ml) water

1 clove garlic, crushed

½ small red onion (50g),
　　chopped finely

½ small lebanese cucumber (60g),
　　seeded, chopped finely

1 tablespoon finely chopped
　　fresh coriander

1 small fresh red thai chilli,
　　chopped finely

1 tablespoon cashews, toasted,
　　chopped coarsely

1　Place noodles in medium bowl of hot water for 10 minutes or until softened; drain well.

2　Thinly slice avocado. Cut carrot into long thin strips. Cut garlic chives into the same lengths as carrot.

3　Cover a board with a damp tea towel. Place one sheet of rice paper in a bowl of warm water until softened; place on tea towel. Place a slice of avocado, some of the carrot, radish, sprouts, a mint leaf, some garlic chives and noodles in the centre of the sheet.

4　Fold bottom half of the rice paper up. Fold in one side; roll over to enclose filling. Repeat with remaining rice paper sheets and ingredients. Place rolls on oven tray lined with plastic wrap; cover with damp absorbent paper and refrigerate until ready to serve.

5　Serve with chilli dipping sauce.

CHILLI DIPPING SAUCE　Bring vinegar, sugar, salt and the water to a boil in small saucepan; boil, uncovered, 2 minutes. Pour vinegar mixture over remaining ingredients in medium bowl. Cool to room temperature.

makes 24

per roll　3.7g fat; 388kJ (93 cal)

TIPS　The dipping sauce can be made a day ahead; keep covered in refrigerator.

The rolls can be made up to four hours ahead. Keep fresh by covering with damp absorbent paper.

polenta with grilled banana chillies

PREPARATION TIME   **COOKING TIME**

2 cups (500ml) vegetable stock

2 cups (500ml) water

1½ cups (250g) instant polenta

20g butter

3 egg yolks

¾ cup (60g) finely grated
 parmesan cheese

3 small fresh red thai chillies,
 seeded, chopped finely

6 medium banana chillies (430g),
 halved lengthways

2 tablespoons olive oil

1 clove garlic, crushed

BASIL DRESSING

1 cup firmly packed fresh basil leaves

⅓ cup (80ml) extra virgin olive oil

1½ tablespoons red wine vinegar

1 clove garlic, crushed

1 teaspoon dijon mustard

1 teaspoon caster sugar

1 Lightly oil 23cm-square slab pan. Bring stock and the water to a
  boil in large saucepan. Add polenta; cook, stirring, about 2 minutes
  or until liquid is absorbed and mixture thickens.

2 Stir in butter, egg yolks, cheese and red thai chilli. Spread polenta
  evenly into prepared pan; cool. Refrigerate about 3 hours or until firm.

3 Brush banana chillies with combined oil and garlic; cook on heated
  grill plate until browned lightly and tender.

4 Turn polenta onto board, trim edges; cut into quarters, then cut each
  quarter into two triangles. Cook polenta on heated oiled grill plate (or
  pan fry or barbecue) until browned on both sides.

5 Serve chilli with polenta; drizzle with basil dressing.
  BASIL DRESSING Blend or process ingredients until almost smooth.

serves 4
per serving 41.7g fat; 2811kJ (671 cal)
TIP Polenta is suitable to freeze before grilling.

goats cheese and garlic bruschetta

PREPARATION TIME   **COOKING TIME**

1 Cut bread into 16 x 1cm-thick slices. Brush one side of bread with combined oil and garlic. Grill bread until browned lightly on both sides.
2 Using a hot, wet knife, slice cheese thinly. Divide cheese evenly among toasted bread. (If cheese is too soft to slice, spread it on the toast, instead.)
3 Top bruschetta with onion, extra olive oil, pepper and rocket leaves.

makes 16
per bruschetta 9.2g fat; 590kJ (141 cal)
TIP Recipe is best made close to serving.

350g loaf ciabatta
¼ cup (60ml) olive oil
2 cloves garlic, crushed
300g goats cheese
¼ small red onion (25g), sliced thinly
2 tablespoons olive oil, extra
50g baby rocket leaves

bruschetta with eggplant and olive topping

PREPARATION TIME   **COOKING TIME**

1 tablespoon virgin olive oil

1 small white onion (80g),
  chopped finely

2 cloves garlic, crushed

1 trimmed celery stalk (100g),
  chopped finely

150g char-grilled eggplant,
  chopped finely

150g roasted red capsicum,
  chopped finely

¼ cup (40g) pitted black olives,
  chopped coarsely

1 tablespoon drained baby capers

2 tablespoons toasted pine nuts

¼ cup finely shredded fresh basil

350g loaf ciabatta

2 tablespoons virgin olive oil, extra

1 Heat oil in medium frying pan; cook onion, garlic and celery until soft. Transfer onion mixture to medium bowl.

2 Add eggplant, capsicum, olives, capers, pine nuts and basil to onion mixture; mix well.

3 Cut bread on slight angle into eight slices. Brush one side of bread slices with the extra oil; grill on both sides until toasted.

4 Top toast with eggplant mixture and sprinkle with extra basil leaves, if desired.

serves 4

per serving 21.5g fat; 1735kJ (414 cal)

TIPS Eggplant mixture can be made several hours ahead. Toast bread close to serving.

calamari stuffed with fetta and chilli

PREPARATION TIME

COOKING TIME

8 whole calamari, with tentacles (600g)

400g firm fetta cheese

1 teaspoon dried chilli flakes

2 tablespoons finely chopped
  fresh oregano

2 tablespoons olive oil

2 teaspoons finely grated lemon rind

2 tablespoons lemon juice

2 tablespoons finely chopped
  fresh oregano, extra

1 clove garlic, crushed

¼ cup (60ml) olive oil

1 To clean calamari, pull gently on the tentacles to remove. Cut tentacles off below the eyes; discard eyes, the small black beak in the centre of the tentacles and entrails. Remove the clear quill from inside the body. Dip fingers into salt, then remove the side flaps and dark membrane. (The salt gives a better grip.) Rinse well and pat dry.

2 Mash cheese, chilli, oregano and oil together in small bowl. Fill calamari tubes with cheese mixture. Use toothpicks to secure opening. Place calamari and tentacles in shallow dish.

3 Combine remaining ingredients in medium jug. Pour over calamari; cover and refrigerate 3 hours, turning occasionally.

4 Cook calamari and tentacles on heated lightly oiled grill plate (or grill or barbecue) about 3 minutes on each side or until browned and cheese is heated through.

serves 8
per calamari 23.4g fat; 1123kJ (268 cal)

olive and cheese fritters

PREPARATION TIME   **COOKING TIME**

1 Dissolve yeast in the warm water in medium jug. Place flour and salt in large bowl, gradually stir in yeast mixture to form a sticky, wet batter. Cover, stand in warm place about 1 hour or until doubled in size.
2 Stir in olives, anchovy, tomato, cheese, onion and garlic.
3 Deep-fry heaped teaspoons of mixture in hot oil, in batches, about 3 minutes or until golden and cooked through.
4 Drain on absorbent paper; sprinkle with sea salt, if desired. Stand 2 minutes before serving.

makes 40
per fritter 2.1g fat; 214kJ (51 cal)
TIP Recipe best cooked just before serving.

2 teaspoons (7g) dried yeast
1 cup (250ml) warm water
2 cups (300g) plain flour
½ teaspoon salt
¼ cup (40g) pitted black olives, chopped coarsely
4 anchovy fillets, drained, chopped finely
4 sun-dried tomatoes, drained, chopped finely
200g bocconcini cheese, chopped finely
1 small white onion (80g), chopped finely
2 cloves garlic, crushed
vegetable oil for deep-frying

curry puffs with cucumber mint raita

PREPARATION TIME   **COOKING TIME**

1 tablespoon vegetable oil

2 cloves garlic, crushed

1 medium brown onion (150g),
   chopped finely

2 small fresh red thai chillies,
   chopped finely

½ teaspoon ground turmeric

2 teaspoons ground cumin

200g pork mince

1 medium potato (200g),
   chopped finely

¼ cup (30g) frozen peas

6 sheets frozen ready rolled
   puff pastry

vegetable oil, extra,
   for deep-frying

CUCUMBER MINT RAITA

1 cup (280g) thick yogurt

1 lebanese cucumber (130g),
   seeded, chopped finely

2 tablespoons coarsely chopped
   fresh mint

½ teaspoon ground cumin

1 tablespoon lime juice

1 Heat oil in large non-stick frying pan; add garlic, onion, chilli, turmeric and cumin, cook, stirring, until onion is soft. Add pork and potato; cook, stirring, until pork is well browned and potato is cooked through. Add peas; remove from heat, cool.

2 Using 8cm cutter, cut pastry into 36 rounds. Place 2 teaspoons of mixture in centre of each round. Fold rounds in half, twisting edges together to seal. Repeat with remaining pastry and pork mixture.

3 Deep-fry puffs in hot oil, in batches, until golden brown; drain on absorbent paper.

4 Serve hot with cucumber mint raita.
   CUCUMBER MINT RAITA Combine ingredients in small bowl; mix well.

makes 36

per curry puff 10.2g fat; 637kJ (152 cal)

TIPS Filling can be made a day ahead; puffs can be prepared several hours ahead. Puffs are best cooked just before serving.

char-grilled prawns with mango chilli salsa

PREPARATION TIME   **COOKING TIME**

1kg large uncooked prawns

MANGO CHILLI SALSA

¼ cup (60ml) lime juice

2 small fresh red thai chillies, chopped finely

¼ cup (60ml) olive oil

2 teaspoons fish sauce

2 teaspoons grated palm sugar

1 medium mango (400g), chopped coarsely

1 medium green mango (400g), sliced thinly

1 small red onion (100g), sliced thinly

½ cup lightly packed fresh coriander leaves

1 Cook prawns in their shells on heated oiled grill (or barbecue) until browned on both sides and just cooked through. Serve prawns with mango chilli salsa.

MANGO CHILLI SALSA Combine juice, chilli, oil, sauce and sugar in medium bowl; stir until sugar is dissolved. Add mangoes, onion and coriander; toss gently.

serves 4

per serving 14.7g fat; 1383kJ (330 cal)

TIP Salsa can be prepared three hours ahead.

saffron prawns

PREPARATION TIME **COOKING TIME**

1 Peel and devein prawns, leaving tails intact.
2 Sift flour and salt into large bowl; whisk in beer and saffron until smooth.
3 Pat prawns dry with absorbent paper. Dip prawns in batter, in batches; drain excess batter. Deep-fry prawns in hot oil until changed in colour and just cooked through. Remove prawns; drain thoroughly on absorbent paper.
4 Repeat with remaining prawns and batter. Serve immediately with lemon wedges.

1kg uncooked king prawns
1½ cups (225g) plain flour
½ teaspoon salt
1½ cups (375ml) light beer
pinch saffron threads
vegetable oil, for deep-frying
lemon wedges, for serving

serves 8
per serving 5.5g fat; 873kJ (208 cal)
TIP Recipe is best made just before serving.

roasted mediterranean vegetables with chilli-and-herb baked ricotta

PREPARATION TIME 15 MINUTES **COOKING TIME** 1 HOUR

Ricotta that is sold packaged in paper or tubs is not suitable for this recipe. Buy the ricotta in a wedge, by weight, from a delicatessen where it is kept in a plastic colander.

3 baby eggplants (180g),
   halved lengthways
3 small zucchini (270g),
   halved lengthways
2 small red capsicums (450g),
   quartered
cooking-oil spray
2 small red onions (200g), quartered
2 trimmed celery stalks (200g),
   cut into thirds
3 small egg tomatoes (180g), halved
6 cloves garlic, unpeeled
1 teaspoon freshly ground
   black pepper
¼ cup (60ml) extra virgin olive oil
2 tablespoons finely shredded
   fresh basil
1 tablespoon baby capers, drained

CHILLI-AND-HERB BAKED RICOTTA

750g wedge fresh ricotta cheese
1 tablespoon extra virgin olive oil
1 teaspoon freshly ground
   black pepper
½ teaspoon dried chilli flakes
2 tablespoons finely chopped
   fresh oregano

1 Preheat oven to hot.
2 Place eggplant, zucchini and capsicum, in single layer, in large shallow baking dish; spray with cooking-oil spray. Roast, uncovered, in hot oven about 1 hour or until vegetables are brown and tender.
3 Meanwhile, place onion, celery, tomato and garlic, in single layer, in another large shallow baking dish; spray with cooking-oil spray. Roast, uncovered, in hot oven, with vegetable mixture, about 15 minutes or until brown and tender.
4 Sprinkle both vegetable dishes with pepper; drizzle with olive oil. Top with basil and capers; serve with chilli-and-herb baked ricotta.
   CHILLI-AND-HERB BAKED RICOTTA Place ricotta on oven tray lined with baking paper. Drizzle with oil; sprinkle with pepper and half of the chilli. Bake, uncovered, in hot oven, about 15 minutes or until warmed through. Sprinkle with oregano and remaining chilli; place ricotta under hot grill until browned lightly.

serves 8
per serving 20.4g fat; 1061kJ (253 cal)

spicy crab and prawn fritters

PREPARATION TIME   **COOKING TIME**

650g large uncooked prawns

2 x 170g cans crab meat, drained

1 tablespoon red curry paste

1 egg

2 green onions, chopped coarsely

2 tablespoons coarsely chopped
fresh coriander

2 teaspoons coarsely chopped
fresh lemon grass

1 small fresh red thai chilli, seeded,
chopped coarsely

2 tablespoons peanut oil

CHILLI LIME DIPPING SAUCE

2 tablespoons lime juice

2 tablespoons water

2 teaspoons fish sauce

2 teaspoons sugar

1 kaffir lime leaf, shredded finely

1 small fresh red thai chilli, seeded,
chopped finely

1   Shell and devein prawns; blend or process with crab, paste, egg,
onion, coriander, lemon grass and chilli until just combined. Using
hands, shape level tablespoons of mixture into fritter shapes.

2   Heat oil in large frying pan; cook fritters, in batches, until golden brown
and cooked through, drain on absorbent paper. Serve fritters with chilli
lime dipping sauce.

CHILLI LIME DIPPING SAUCE   Place ingredients in small bowl; whisk
until sugar dissolves.

makes 30

per fritter 1.7g fat; 131kJ (31 cal)

TIPS To save time, buy 400g of shelled uncooked prawns.

If you can't find a kaffir lime leaf, use 1 teaspoon of finely grated
lime rind.

chicken and ham patties

PREPARATION TIME   **COOKING TIME**

1 Combine all ingredients, except the oil, in large bowl. Shape
  ¼-cups of mixture into flat patties.
2 Heat oil in medium frying pan; cook patties, in batches, until
  browned on both sides and cooked through.
3 Serve patties with dipping sauce and rocket leaves, if desired.
  DIPPING SAUCE Combine sauces in small bowl.

serves 6
per serving 25.3g fat; 1789kJ (427 cal)
TIP Patties can be prepared several hours ahead.

1kg chicken mince
250g sliced ham, chopped finely
2 tablespoons finely chopped
  fresh coriander
1 clove garlic, crushed
3 green onions, chopped finely
1 cup (70g) stale breadcrumbs
¼ cup (60ml) olive oil

DIPPING SAUCE

2 tablespoons salt-reduced
  soy sauce
1 tablespoon sweet chilli sauce

spring rolls with chilli plum sauce

PREPARATION TIME 30 MINUTES (PLUS STANDING TIME) **COOKING TIME** 30 MINUTES

6 dried shiitake mushrooms

200g pork mince

2 chinese cabbage leaves,
   shredded finely

1 trimmed celery stalk (100g),
   shredded finely

1 small carrot (70g), grated finely

½ cup (40g) bean sprouts

1 green onion, sliced thinly

1 tablespoon finely chopped
   fresh coriander

1 teaspoon peanut oil

1 clove garlic, crushed

1 tablespoon light soy sauce

1 tablespoon oyster sauce

36 x 12.5mm square mini
   spring roll wrappers

1 egg, beaten lightly

vegetable oil for deep-frying

CHILLI PLUM SAUCE

1 cup (250ml) plum sauce

1 tablespoon soy sauce

3cm piece fresh ginger (15g),
   grated finely

1 small fresh red thai chilli,
   seeded, chopped finely

1 Place mushrooms in heatproof bowl; cover with boiling water, stand 20 minutes. Drain mushrooms; discard stems, chop finely.

2 Combine mushrooms with remaining ingredients, except wrappers, egg and vegetable oil, in large bowl; mix well.

3 For each roll, place 2 teaspoons of filling across one corner of wrapper. Brush edges of wrapper with a little egg, tuck in ends and roll up to enclose filling.

4 Deep-fry spring rolls, in batches, in hot oil until golden brown and cooked through; drain on absorbent paper.

5 Serve spring rolls with chilli plum sauce.

CHILLI PLUM SAUCE Combine ingredients in small bowl.

makes 36

per spring roll 2.4g fat; 265kJ (63 cal)

TIPS The filling can be made several hours ahead.

Rolls can be made up to two hours ahead. Place in single layer on tray lined with plastic wrap; cover and refrigerate. Deep-fry just before serving.

Curl up and get comfortable, it's soup season. These mouth-watering recipes, including roasted pumpkin soup and ham and lentil soup, are full of robust flavours, while others, such as vietnamese prawn soup and chicken and noodles in broth, are infused with the ginger, garlic and soy influences of Asia – just the thing to ward off the chill of winter. Thick and chunky or smooth and creamy, a generous helping of these more-ish soups will satisfy any hunger.

tuscan bean soup

PREPARATION TIME 15 MINUTES **COOKING TIME** 2 HOURS 35 MINUTES

2 tablespoons olive oil

3 medium brown onions (450g),
   chopped coarsely

2 cloves garlic, crushed

200g piece speck, bacon or
   pancetta, chopped coarsely

2 medium carrots (240g),
   chopped coarsely

2 trimmed celery stalks (200g),
   chopped coarsely

2 x 400g cans tomatoes

¼ medium savoy cabbage (375g),
   shredded coarsely

1 medium zucchini (120g),
   chopped coarsely

2 sprigs fresh thyme

2 cups (500ml) beef stock

2 litres (8 cups) water

400g can borlotti beans,
   rinsed, drained

6 thick slices ciabatta

1 Heat oil in large saucepan. Add onion, garlic and speck; cook, stirring, about 5 minutes or until onion is soft.

2 Add carrot, celery, undrained crushed tomatoes, cabbage, zucchini, thyme, stock and the water. Bring to a boil; then simmer, uncovered, 2 hours.

3 Add beans; simmer, uncovered, 20 minutes.

4 Meanwhile, toast or grill bread. Place a slice of bread in the base of six serving bowls, top with soup. Drizzle with extra olive oil, if desired.

serves 6
per serving 8.9g fat; 1272kJ (304 cal)

mushroom soup with goats cheese croûtes

PREPARATION TIME   **COOKING TIME**

1 Melt 50g of the butter in large saucepan; add mushrooms, except
   enoki mushrooms, cook, stirring, until softened. Remove from pan.
2 Heat remaining butter in same pan. Add onion and garlic; cook,
   stirring, until onion is soft. Add flour, stir for 1 minute. Stir in stock and
   the water, return half of mushrooms to pan. Bring to a boil; simmer,
   uncovered, 30 minutes.
3 Blend soup, in batches, until smooth. Return to pan; whisk in
   sour cream and remaining half of mushrooms, bring to a boil;
   remove from heat.
4 Heat oil in small frying pan; cook enoki mushrooms over high
   heat until browned lightly.
5 Meanwhile, toast bread slices under hot grill until lightly browned;
   turn, spread with goats cheese, grill until cheese is heated.
6 Divide soup among serving bowls, top with enoki mushrooms;
   serve with goats cheese croûtes.

serves 6
per serving 29.9g fat; 1841kJ (440 cal)
TIPS Soup can be made a day ahead.
Make croûtes just before serving.

125g butter
400g button mushrooms,
   sliced thinly
300g medium cap mushrooms,
   sliced thinly
300g swiss brown mushrooms,
   sliced thinly
3 medium brown onions (450g),
   sliced thinly
2 cloves garlic, crushed
⅓ cup (50g) plain flour
2 cups (500ml) chicken stock
1.5 litres (6 cups) water
½ cup (120g) sour cream
2 teaspoons olive oil
100g enoki mushrooms
1 small french bread stick,
   cut into 12 slices
150g log goats cheese

vietnamese prawn soup

PREPARATION TIME   **COOKING TIME**

500g uncooked king prawns

2cm piece fresh ginger (10g),
    sliced thinly

1 teaspoon black peppercorns

2 cloves garlic, crushed

2 large fresh red chillies,
    seeded, sliced thinly

1 stalk lemon grass, sliced coarsely

3 litres (12 cups) water

400g fresh rice noodles

¼ cup (60ml) lemon juice

⅓ cup (80ml) fish sauce,
    approximately

2 green onions, sliced thinly

⅓ cup firmly packed fresh
    coriander leaves

¼ cup firmly packed fresh
    mint leaves

1 Peel and devein prawns, discard heads. Place prawn shells, ginger, peppercorns, garlic, half of the chilli, lemon grass and the water in large saucepan. Bring to a boil, reduce heat; simmer, uncovered, 20 minutes. Strain stock; return liquid to clean saucepan.

2 Add prawns to stock; simmer, covered, about 3 minutes or until prawns are changed in colour.

3 Meanwhile, pour boiling water over rice noodles in bowl; drain.

4 Add lemon juice to stock, gradually add fish sauce to taste. Divide prawns and noodles evenly among serving bowls, top with stock, green onion, herbs and remaining chilli.

serves 6

per serving 0.41g fat; 221kJ (53 cal)

TIP Recipe best made just before serving.

spring vegetable soup

PREPARATION TIME   **COOKING TIMES**

1 tablespoon olive oil

1 small brown onion (80g),
   chopped finely

1 clove garlic, crushed

350g baby carrots, sliced thickly

3 cups (750ml) chicken stock

2 cups (500ml) water

¼ cup (55g) farfalline, risoni
   or any small soup pasta

200g asparagus, sliced thickly

1 cup (120g) frozen peas

⅓ cup (25g) coarsely grated
   parmesan cheese

1 tablespoon finely chopped
   fresh chives

1 Heat oil in large saucepan, add onion and garlic, cook, stirring, until onion is soft. Add carrot, cook, stirring, 2 minutes.

2 Add stock and the water; bring to a boil. Stir in pasta and simmer soup, uncovered, about 8 minutes or until pasta is tender. Return to a boil, add asparagus and frozen peas; simmer, uncovered, until tender.

3 Serve sprinkled with cheese and chives.

serves 4

per serving 7.8g fat; 786kJ (188 cal)

TIP This recipe can be made a day ahead. If the soup thickens on standing, thin with a little more water or stock.

easy beef and barley soup

PREPARATION TIME   **COOKING TIME**

1 Trim fat from beef, cut into 1cm pieces. Heat oil in large saucepan; add onion and garlic, cook, stirring, until onion is soft.

2 Add beef, barley, pepper, stock and the water; bring to a boil, simmer, covered, 3 hours, stirring occasionally. Stir in parsley.

serves 6
per serving 22g fat; 1774kJ (423 cal)

1kg gravy beef
1 tablespoon olive oil
2 medium brown onions (300g), chopped finely
2 cloves garlic, crushed
¾ cup (150g) pearl barley
2 teaspoons cracked black pepper
2 cups (500ml) beef stock
1.5 litres (6 cups) water
⅓ cup coarsely chopped fresh flat-leaf parsley

ham and lentil soup

PREPARATION TIME 15 MINUTES **COOKING TIME** 1 HOUR 15 MINUTES

2 tablespoons olive oil

1 medium brown onion (150g),
    chopped finely

2 medium carrots (240g),
    chopped finely

2 trimmed celery stalks (200g),
    chopped finely

2 cups (400g) brown lentils

500g ham hock

3 litres (12 cups) water

2 cloves garlic, peeled

2 bay leaves

¼ cup coarsely chopped fresh
    flat-leaf parsley

1 Heat oil in large saucepan; add onion, carrot and celery, cook, stirring, about 5 minutes or until softened.

2 Add remaining ingredients, except parsley; bring to a boil. Reduce heat, simmer, covered, about 1 hour or until lentils and vegetables are tender.

3 Remove ham hock. Discard skin and slice meat. Remove and discard bay leaves.

4 Blend or process half of the soup, in batches, until smooth. Return soup to pan with meat, stir over medium heat until hot.

5 Serve sprinkled with parsley.

serves 6
per serving 12.5g fat; 1470kJ (351 cal)
TIP Recipe can be made a day ahead. Thin with water on reheating, if necessary.

roast pumpkin soup with cheese croûtes

PREPARATION 15 MINUTES **COOKING TIME** 45 MINUTES

1kg grey-skinned pumpkin,
   peeled, chopped coarsely
3 cloves garlic, peeled
1 medium brown onion (150g),
   chopped coarsely
1 tablespoon olive oil
3 cups (750ml) chicken stock
⅔ cup (160ml) cream
1 teaspoon finely chopped fresh thyme

CHEESE CROUTES

¼ cup (60ml) olive oil
1 tablespoon wholegrain mustard
2 teaspoons finely chopped
   fresh thyme
1 small french bread stick, sliced thinly
⅓ cup (25g) finely grated
   parmesan cheese

1 Preheat oven to moderately hot.
2 Combine pumpkin, garlic and onion in large baking dish; drizzle with oil. Roast, uncovered, in moderately hot oven about 30 minutes or until soft.
3 Blend or process roasted vegetables with stock until smooth. Place mixture in large saucepan, stir over heat until hot; stir in cream and thyme.
4 Serve soup with cheese croûtes.
   CHEESE CROUTES Combine oil, mustard and thyme in small bowl; brush mixture over bread slices. Place slices on oven tray. Bake in moderately hot oven 5 minutes; sprinkle with cheese and bake 3 minutes or until crisp.

serves 4
per serving 38.1g fat; 2291kJ (547 cal)
TIPS The soup can be made a day ahead.
The croûtes are best made close to serving.

greek lamb and lima bean soup

PREPARATION TIME   **COOKING TIME**

1 Place beans in medium bowl, cover with water; stand overnight, drain.
2 Heat oil in large saucepan, cook lamb, in batches, until browned all over. Add onion, garlic, carrot and celery to same pan; cook, stirring, until softened.
3 Return lamb to pan with beans, stock and the water; bring to a boil. Simmer, covered, 1 hour, skimming surface occasionally.
4 Remove lamb shanks from pan. When cool enough to handle, remove meat from bones, discard bones; shred meat. Return meat to pan with undrained tomatoes, simmer, covered, 1 hour. Stir in dill and juice.

serves 8
per serving 8g fat; 783kJ (187 cal)
TIP Recipe can be made two days ahead.

1 cup (200g) dried lima beans
2 tablespoons olive oil
3 lamb shanks (750g)
2 medium brown onions (300g),0
   chopped finely
1 clove garlic, crushed
2 medium carrots (240g),
   chopped finely
2 trimmed celery stalks (200g),
   chopped finely
2 cups (500ml) chicken stock
1 litre (4 cups) water
400g can chopped tomatoes
¼ cup coarsely chopped fresh dill
2 tablespoons lemon juice

chicken and noodles in broth

PREPARATION TIME   **COOKING TIME**

3 cups (750ml) chicken stock

3 cups (750ml) boiling water

3cm piece fresh ginger (15g),
   grated finely

2 cloves garlic, crushed

2 tablespoons soy sauce

2 small fresh red thai chillies,
   seeded, sliced thinly

4 single chicken breast fillets (680g)

450g hokkien noodles

200g asparagus, quartered
   lengthways

4 green onions, sliced thinly

1   Combine stock, the water, ginger, garlic, sauce and chilli in large saucepan; cover, bring to a boil.

2   Add chicken, simmer, covered, about 15 minutes or until chicken is just cooked through. Remove chicken from stock mixture.

3   Return stock mixture to a boil, add noodles, use a fork to separate noodles. Add asparagus; simmer, uncovered, until just tender.

4   Meanwhile, slice chicken thickly. Divide noodles and stock mixture among serving bowls. Top with chicken, asparagus and onion.

5   Serve with extra soy sauce and chilli, if desired.

serves 4

per serving 6g fat; 2158kJ (515 cal)

TIP   Recipe is best made just before serving.

beef in asian broth

PREPARATION TIME   **COOKING TIME**

1.5 litres (6 cups) water

410g can beef consommé

3cm piece fresh ginger (15g),
  grated finely

2 tablespoons salt-reduced
  soy sauce

1 teaspoon sesame oil

100g bean thread noodles

500g beef rump, trimmed,
  sliced thinly

1 small red capsicum (150g),
  sliced thinly

200g fresh baby corn

1 green onion, sliced thinly

500g baby bok choy,
  chopped coarsely

2 cups (160g) bean sprouts

1 small fresh red thai chilli,
  sliced thinly

1 Combine the water, consommé, ginger, sauce and oil in large saucepan;
   bring to a boil. Add noodles; using fork, separate noodles. Reduce heat;
   simmer, uncovered, until noodles are just tender.
2 Add remaining ingredients; stir until mixture is heated through and beef
   is cooked as desired.

serves 4
per serving 8.5g fat; 1216kJ (291 cal)

chicken and vegetable soup

PREPARATION TIME   **COOKING TIME**

1 Heat oil in large saucepan. Add leek; cook, stirring, about
   2 minutes or until leek is soft. Add carrot and celery; cook,
   stirring, about 2 minutes or until vegetables are softened slightly.

2 Rinse chicken under cold water, pat dry with absorbent paper.
   Remove skin and excess fat from chicken.

3 Add chicken to pan with garlic, consommé and the water. Bring
   to a boil, simmer, uncovered, about 45 minutes or until chicken
   is cooked through.

4 Remove chicken from soup, cool slightly. Remove meat from
   chicken; discard bones. Chop meat coarsely, return to soup
   with beans. Bring to a boil, then simmer, uncovered, until beans
   are tender. Stir in parsley.

serves 6
per serving 27.4g fat; 1668kJ (399 cal)
   This recipe can be made a day ahead; skim solidified fat
from the surface, then add beans and parsley when reheating.

1 tablespoon olive oil
1 large leek (500g), halved,
   sliced thinly
3 small carrots (200g), halved,
   sliced thinly
2 trimmed celery stalks (200g),
   sliced thinly
1.8kg whole chicken
6 cloves garlic, peeled
410g can chicken consommé
2.75 litres (11 cups) water
200g green beans,
   chopped coarsely
⅓ cup finely chopped fresh
   flat-leaf parsley

seafood soup with capsicum rouille

PREPARATION TIME 45 MINUTES **COOKING TIME** 30 MINUTES

1 tablespoon olive oil

1 medium leek (350g),
   sliced thinly

1 small brown onion (80g),
   chopped finely

1 medium fennel (300g),
   sliced thinly

2 cloves garlic, crushed

pinch saffron threads

400g can crushed tomatoes

3 cups (750ml) fish stock

2 cups (500ml) water

500g medium uncooked prawns

1 uncooked blue swimmer crab

500g small mussels

700g firm white fish fillets,
   cut into 3cm pieces

⅓ cup coarsely chopped fresh
   flat-leaf parsley

1 small french bread stick,
   sliced thinly, toasted

CAPSICUM ROUILLE

1 medium red capsicum (200g)

1 long fresh red chilli, seeded,
   chopped coarsely

1 clove garlic, crushed

½ cup (35g) stale breadcrumbs

2 tablespoons lemon juice

1 tablespoon water

½ cup (125ml) olive oil

1 Heat oil in large saucepan, add leek, onion, fennel and garlic; cook, stirring, about 10 minutes or until softened.

2 Add saffron, undrained tomatoes, stock and the water; bring to a boil. Reduce heat; simmer, uncovered, 10 minutes. Blend mixture, in batches, until smooth.

3 Return mixture to pan; bring to a boil.

4 Peel and devein prawns; clean crab and cut into six pieces. Add mussels and fish to tomato mixture in pan; simmer, covered, 5 minutes or until mussels open (discard any that do not). Add prawns and crab pieces; simmer, covered, until just cooked. Stir in parsley.

5 Serve soup with toasted bread and capsicum rouille.
   CAPSICUM ROUILLE Quarter capsicum; discard seeds and membranes. Roast under grill or in very hot oven, skin-side up, until skin blisters and blackens. Cover pieces in plastic wrap for 5 minutes, then peel skin. Blend capsicum with remaining ingredients, except oil, until smooth. With motor operating, gradually add oil in thin stream. Blend until mixture thickens.

serves 6

per serving 27g fat; 2176kJ (520 cal)

TIPS Rouille is traditionally made with chillies and is quite hot. This is a milder, sweeter version with capsicum. It can be made a day ahead. The soup base, without seafood, also can be made a day ahead.

MAINS

From the casual food of summer — quick barbecues, stir-fries and pan-fries — to the comfort food of winter — slow-cooked casseroles and roasts — there's a recipe here to suit every occasion. Beef, lamb, pork, poultry, seafood and vegetarian are cooked in every way imaginable. There's bowl food, such as beef coconut curry, casual food, such as chicken pitta pockets, frittatas, risottos, roasts and a twist on an old-favourite, the steak sandwich.

standing rib roast with roast vegetables

PREPARATION TIME   **COOKING TIME**

1.2kg standing beef rib roast

¼ cup (60ml) olive oil

2 teaspoons cracked black pepper

500g baby new potatoes

500g pumpkin, chopped coarsely

500g kumara, chopped coarsely

½ cup (125ml) brandy

1½ cups (375ml) beef stock

1 tablespoon cornflour

¼ cup (60ml) water

1 tablespoon finely chopped
   fresh chives

1 Preheat oven to moderately hot.

2 Brush beef with 1 tablespoon of the oil; sprinkle with black pepper. Heat 1 tablespoon of the oil in large, shallow, flameproof baking dish; cook beef, uncovered, over high heat until browned all over.

3 Place dish in moderately hot oven; roast, uncovered, about 45 minutes or until beef is cooked as desired.

4 Meanwhile, heat remaining oil in another large flameproof baking dish; cook potato, stirring, over high heat until browned lightly. Add pumpkin and kumara, place dish in oven; roast, uncovered, in moderately hot oven about 35 minutes or until vegetables are browned.

5 Reduce oven to slow. Place beef on vegetables, cover; return to oven to keep warm. Drain juices from beef baking dish into medium saucepan, add brandy; bring to a boil. Add stock and blended cornflour and water; cook, stirring, until sauce boils and thickens slightly. Stir in chives; pour into medium heatproof jug.

6 Serve roast and vegetables on large platter; accompany with sauce.

serves 4

per serving 36.7g fat; 3286kJ (785 cal)

TIP This recipe is best made close to serving.

cajun steaks with mango salsa

PREPARATION TIME   **COOKING TIME**

1½ teaspoons cajun seasoning

4 beef steaks (500g)

4 thick slices crusty bread

100g mesclun

MANGO SALSA

1 small mango (300g),
chopped coarsely

2 medium tomatoes (300g),
seeded, chopped coarsely

1 small red onion (100g),
chopped finely

1 clove garlic, crushed

2 tablespoons finely shredded
fresh basil

1 tablespoon balsamic vinegar

1. Make mango salsa.
2. Sprinkle seasoning over beef; cook on heated oiled grill plate (or grill or barbecue) until browned both sides and cooked as desired.
3. Meanwhile, toast bread both sides. Divide bread among serving plates; top with mesclun, beef and mango salsa.

MANGO SALSA Combine ingredients in medium bowl.

serves 4

per serving 7.3g fat; 1227kJ (294 cal)

TIP We used thinly sliced boneless beef sirloin for this recipe, however, rump steak or scotch fillet also are suitable.

beef coconut curry

PREPARATION TIME   **COOKING TIME**

1 Heat half of the oil in wok or large frying pan; stir-fry beef, in batches, until browned all over.
2 Heat remaining oil in same wok; stir-fry onion until soft. Add ginger, garlic and paste; stir-fry until fragrant.
3 Stir in coconut milk; bring to a boil. Reduce heat, return beef to wok with capsicum and beans; stir-fry until vegetables are just tender.

serves 4
per serving 43.5g fat; 2329kJ (557 cal)
SERVING SUGGESTION Serve with steamed white rice and pappadums, if desired.

2 tablespoons peanut oil
500g beef rump steak,
    sliced thinly
1 medium brown onion (150g),
    sliced thinly
3cm piece fresh ginger (15g),
    grated finely
1 clove garlic, crushed
⅓ cup (100g) mild curry paste
1⅔ cups (400ml) coconut milk
1 medium yellow capsicum (200g),
    sliced thinly
150g green beans, halved

saltimbocca with risotto milanese

PREPARATION TIME   **COOKING TIME**

8 veal steaks (640g)

4 slices prosciutto (60g),
   halved widthways

8 fresh sage leaves

½ cup (40g) finely grated
   pecorino cheese

40g butter

1 cup (250ml) dry white wine

1 tablespoon coarsely chopped
   fresh sage, extra

RISOTTO MILANESE

1½ cups (375ml) water

2 cups (500ml) chicken stock

½ cup (125ml) dry white wine

¼ teaspoon saffron threads

20g butter

1 large brown onion (200g),
   chopped finely

2 cups (400g) arborio rice

¼ cup (20g) finely grated
   parmesan cheese

1 Place veal on a board. Place one piece of prosciutto, one sage leaf and one-eighth of the cheese on each piece of veal; fold in half to enclose filling, secure with a toothpick or small skewer.

2 Make risotto milanese.

3 Melt half of the butter in medium non-stick frying pan; cook veal, in batches, until browned on both sides and cooked through. Remove from pan; cover to keep warm.

4 Pour wine into same frying pan; bring to a boil. Boil, uncovered, until wine reduces by half. Stir in remaining butter, then sage.

5 Divide risotto milanese and saltimbocca among serving plates; drizzle saltimbocca with sauce and accompany with steamed green beans, if desired.

RISOTTO MILANESE Place the water, stock, wine and saffron in medium saucepan; bring to a boil. Reduce heat; simmer, covered. Heat butter in another medium saucepan; add onion, cook, stirring, until softened. Add rice; stir to coat rice in onion mixture. Stir in ½ cup of the simmering stock mixture; cook, stirring, over low heat, until liquid is absorbed. Continue adding stock mixture, in ½-cup batches, stirring until liquid is absorbed after each addition. The total cooking time should be about 25 minutes or until rice is just tender. Stir the cheese gently into risotto.

serves 4

per serving 22.4g fat; 3338kJ (797 cal)

TIPS Cook saltimbocca and risotto close to serving.
Veal can be prepared several hours ahead.

beef and mixed mushroom stir-fry

PREPARATION TIME 5 MINUTES **COOKING TIME** 20 MINUTES

You can find garlic oil among the other cooking oils on your supermarket shelves.

600g hokkien noodles
¼ cup (60ml) garlic oil
100g button mushrooms, halved
200g flat mushrooms,
    sliced thickly
100g swiss brown mushrooms,
    halved
2 trimmed celery stalks (200g),
    sliced thickly
2 small fresh red thai chillies,
    sliced thinly
750g beef strips
½ cup (125ml) oyster sauce

1 Place noodles in large bowl, cover with boiling water; separate noodles with a fork, drain.

2 Heat half of the oil in wok or large frying pan; stir-fry mushrooms, in batches, until browned. Return mushrooms to wok, add celery and chilli; stir-fry until celery just softens. Remove from wok.

3 Heat remaining oil in same wok; stir-fry beef, in batches, until browned all over. Return beef to wok, add noodles and mushroom mixture with sauce; stir-fry until heated through.

serves 6
per serving 25.1g fat; 2570kJ (615 cal)
TIP Swiss brown mushrooms are also known as cremini or roman mushrooms.

chilli beef stir-fry

PREPARATION TIME   **COOKING TIME**

1 Heat oil in wok or large frying pan; stir-fry beef, in batches, until browned and tender.
2 Add beans to wok; stir-fry until almost tender. Add garlic, chilli and paste; stir-fry until fragrant. Add bok choy, stir-fry until just tender.
3 Meanwhile, place noodles in large bowl, cover with boiling water; separate noodles with a fork, drain.
4 Return beef to wok with stock, noodles and green onion. Stir-fry until hot; add mint and toss well.

serves 4
per serving 27.2g fat; 2416kJ (577 cal)
TIP Recipe is best made just before serving.

¼ cup (60ml) olive oil
700g beef rump steak, sliced thinly
300g green beans,
   cut into 5cm lengths
1 clove garlic, chopped coarsely
2 fresh long red chillies, sliced thinly
⅓ cup (90g) thai chilli jam
   stir-fry paste
350g baby bok choy, quartered
450g hokkien noodles
¼ cup (60ml) beef stock
4 green onions, sliced thinly
⅓ cup firmly packed fresh
   mint leaves

beef, tomato and pea pies

PREPARATION TIME
COOKING TIME

1 tablespoon vegetable oil

1 small brown onion (80g),
    chopped finely

300g beef mince

400g can crushed tomatoes

1 tablespoon tomato paste

2 tablespoons worcestershire
    sauce

½ cup (125ml) beef stock

½ cup (60g) frozen peas

3 sheets ready-rolled puff pastry

1 egg, beaten lightly

1   Heat oil in large saucepan; add onion, cook, stirring, until softened. Add beef; cook, stirring, until changed in colour. Stir in undrained tomatoes, tomato paste, sauce and stock; bring to a boil. Reduce heat, simmer, uncovered, about 20 minutes or until sauce thickens. Stir in peas. Allow to cool.

2   Preheat oven to moderately hot. Oil a six-hole ¾-cup (180ml) texas muffin pan.

3   Cut two 13cm rounds from opposite corners of each pastry sheet; cut two 9cm rounds from remaining corners of each sheet. Place six large rounds in muffin pan holes to cover bases and sides; trim any excess pastry. Lightly prick bases with a fork; refrigerate for 30 minutes. Cover the six small rounds with a damp cloth.

4   Cover pastry-lined muffin pan holes with baking paper; fill holes with uncooked rice or dried beans. Bake, uncovered, in moderately hot oven 10 minutes; remove paper and rice. Cool.

5   Spoon beef filling into holes; brush edges with a little egg. Top pies with small pastry rounds; gently press around edges to seal.

6   Brush pies with remaining egg; bake, uncovered, in moderately hot oven about 15 minutes or until browned lightly. Stand 5 minutes in pan before serving with mashed potato, if desired.

makes 6
per pie 26.9g fat; 1887kJ (451 cal)
TIPS The filling can be made a day ahead.
Pies are best cooked close to serving.

sesame beef and pasta salad

PREPARATION TIME   **COOKING TIME**

500g capellini pasta

1kg beef rump steak, sliced thinly

1 clove garlic, crushed

2 tablespoons sweet chilli sauce

1 tablespoon peanut oil

1 medium yellow capsicum (200g),
   sliced thinly

1 medium carrot (120g),
   sliced thinly

100g trimmed watercress

150g snow peas, trimmed,
   sliced thinly

2 teaspoons sesame seeds,
   toasted

SESAME DRESSING

⅓ cup (80ml) peanut oil

½ teaspoon sesame oil

⅓ cup (80ml) rice vinegar

2 tablespoons light soy sauce

1 tablespoon lemon juice

1 green onion, sliced thinly

1 Cook pasta in large saucepan of boiling water, uncovered, until just tender; drain. Rinse under cold water; drain.

2 Meanwhile, make sesame dressing.

3 Combine beef, garlic and sauce in large bowl. Heat oil in wok or large frying pan; stir-fry beef mixture, in batches, until beef is browned all over and cooked as desired.

4 Place pasta and beef in large bowl with vegetables and sesame dressing; toss gently to combine. Sprinkle with sesame seeds.

SESAME DRESSING Combine ingredients in screw-topped jar; shake well.

serves 6

per serving 25g fat; 2801kJ (670 cal)

TIPS Watercress, also known as winter rocket, is a slightly peppery, dark-green leaf vegetable. It is highly perishable, so must be used as soon as possible after purchase.

Capellini is a thin, rod-shaped pasta, slightly thicker than angel hair pasta. It can be found at your local supermarket.

steak sandwich revisited

PREPARATION TIME   **COOKING TIME**

1 Make chilli tomato jam.

2 Make caramelised leek.

3 Cook beef on heated oiled grill plate (or grill or barbecue) until browned on both sides and cooked as desired.

4 Meanwhile, brush both sides of bread slices with oil; toast both sides under hot grill.

5 Sandwich rocket, beef, chilli tomato jam and caramelised leek between toast slices.

CHILLI TOMATO JAM Heat oil in medium saucepan; cook garlic, stirring, until browned lightly. Add tomato, sauces and sugar; bring to a boil. Reduce heat; simmer, uncovered, about 45 minutes or until mixture thickens. Stand 10 minutes; stir in coriander.

CARAMELISED LEEK Melt butter in medium frying pan; add leek, cook, stirring, until softened. Add sugar and wine; cook, stirring occasionally, about 20 minutes or until leek caramelises.

serves 4

per serving 35.1g fat; 3443kJ (823 cal)

TIPS Scotch fillet steak is also known as rib-eye steak.

We used a loaf of ciabatta, an italian bread, for this recipe.

This recipe is best made close to serving.

Chilli tomato jam can be made up to three days ahead; gently reheat when required.

4 beef scotch fillet steaks (800g)

8 thick slices (320g) crusty white bread

2 tablespoons olive oil

60g rocket leaves, trimmed

CHILLI TOMATO JAM

1 tablespoon olive oil

2 cloves garlic, crushed

4 medium tomatoes (600g), chopped coarsely

1 tablespoon worcestershire sauce

½ cup (125ml) sweet chilli sauce

⅓ cup (75g) firmly packed brown sugar

1 tablespoon coarsely chopped fresh coriander

CARAMELISED LEEK

30g butter

1 medium leek (350g), sliced thinly

2 tablespoons brown sugar

2 tablespoons dry white wine

veal rack with roasted mushroom sauce

PREPARATION TIME   **COOKING TIME**

1kg veal rack

¼ cup (60ml) olive oil

1kg baby new potatoes

300g button mushrooms

150g shimeji or oyster mushrooms

2 cloves garlic, sliced

2 tablespoons grated
   parmesan cheese

2 tablespoons plain flour

1½ cups (375ml) chicken stock

⅓ cup (80ml) cream

2 tablespoons coarsely chopped
   fresh flat-leaf parsley

1 Preheat oven to moderately hot.

2 Place veal on wire rack in shallow flameproof baking dish. Rub veal with 1 tablespoon of the olive oil, sprinkle with salt and pepper. Place dish in moderately hot oven; roast, uncovered, 10 minutes. Place potato in small separate dish; roast potato and veal about 30 minutes or until veal is cooked as desired, brushing it with any pan juices. Remove veal from dish; cover to keep warm.

3 Place mushrooms, garlic and remaining olive oil in the veal baking dish; stir to combine. Roast mushroom mixture and potato about 20 minutes or until potato is tender. Sprinkle potato with parmesan; roast 5 minutes or until cheese is melted.

4 Meanwhile, place mushroom mixture in baking dish over medium heat on stove top; add flour and cook, stirring, about 2 minutes or until bubbling. Gradually stir in stock and any juices collected from veal; cook mixture, stirring, until sauce boils and thickens. Add cream and parsley, stir until heated through.

5 Serve veal with mushroom sauce and potato.

serves 4

per serving 29g fat; 2744kJ (656 cal)

TIP Recipe is best made close to serving.

mediterranean roast beef and vegetables

PREPARATION TIME 15 MINUTES   **COOKING TIME** 1 HOUR 30 MINUTES (PLUS STANDING TIME)

1.5kg piece fresh beef eye
  of silverside
⅓ cup (80ml) olive oil
6 whole baby onions (150g)
3 medium zucchini (360g),
  halved lengthways
6 medium egg tomatoes (450g),
  halved lengthways
3 finger eggplants (180g),
  halved lengthways
2 medium yellow capsicums (400g),
  quartered
2 tablespoons balsamic vinegar
2 tablespoons shredded fresh basil
2 tablespoons chopped
  fresh tarragon
1 tablespoon drained baby capers

1 Preheat oven to moderately hot.
2 Rub beef with 2 teaspoons of the olive oil; sprinkle with salt and
  pepper. Heat a further 1 tablespoon of the oil in a large flameproof
  baking dish; add beef and cook until browned all over. Add onion
  to dish, transfer dish to oven; roast, uncovered, in moderately hot
  oven 20 minutes.
3 Place prepared vegetables around beef in dish. Roast, uncovered,
  about 40 minutes or until beef is cooked as desired. Remove beef
  from dish, cover with foil and stand 10 minutes.
4 Meanwhile, increase oven temperature to very hot. Return vegetables
  to oven, roast 10 minutes or until browned and tender.
5 Drizzle vegetables with remaining oil, vinegar, herbs and capers. Serve
  thinly sliced beef with vegetable mixture.

serves 6
per serving 24.5g fat; 1961kJ (468 cal)
TIP Recipe is best made close to serving.

veal cutlets with mustard sauce

PREPARATION TIME   **COOKING TIME**

1 Sprinkle veal with pepper. Heat oil in large non-stick frying pan, add
   veal; cook until browned on both sides and cooked as desired.
   Remove veal from pan, cover to keep warm.
2 Add wine to pan; bring to a boil. Add stock to pan; return to a
   boil and simmer, uncovered, about 15 minutes, or until reduced
   to ⅔ cup (160ml).
3 Remove from heat, stir in the cream and mustard.
4 Serve veal with mustard sauce; accompany with steamed green
   beans and baby carrots, if desired.

4 veal cutlets (500g),
   french trimmed
1 tablespoon olive oil
¾ cup (180ml) dry white wine
1½ cups (375ml) chicken stock
⅓ cup (80ml) cream
1 tablespoon wholegrain mustard

serves 4
per serving 15.9g fat; 1220kJ (292 cal)
TIPS This recipe is best made just before serving.
Ask your butcher to french trim the cutlets for you.

beef and red wine casserole

PREPARATION TIME 30 MINUTES **COOKING TIME** 3 HOURS

1.5kg beef chuck steak

2 tablespoons olive oil

5 cloves garlic

200g speck, cut into thick strips

6 small carrots (420g)

6 baby onions (150g)

2 trimmed celery stalks (200g),
   chopped coarsely

1 cup (250ml) dry red wine

1 cup (250ml) beef consommé
   or stock

1 cup (250ml) water

2 tablespoons plain flour

⅓ cup (80ml) water, extra

1 Preheat oven to slow.

2 Cut beef into 4cm cubes. Heat oil in large, 4-litre (16-cup), flameproof casserole dish. Cook beef in small batches until well browned all over. (It is important to brown beef well at this stage for good flavour and colour.) Remove beef from dish.

3 Crush two cloves of the garlic, leaving three cloves whole. Add garlic, speck, carrot, onion and celery; cook, stirring, about 5 minutes or until browned lightly.

4 Stir in wine; simmer, uncovered, until reduced by half. Add consommé and the water, bring to a boil. Return beef to dish and cook, covered, in slow oven about 2½ hours or until beef is tender, stirring halfway through cooking.

5 Transfer beef and vegetables to serving dish; cover to keep warm. Whisk the blended flour and extra water into liquid in dish; stir over heat until mixture boils and thickens. Pour over beef and vegetables in dish.

serves 8

per serving 16.4g fat; 1604kJ (383 cal)

TIP Can be made up to three days ahead.

roast lamb with tomato and potatoes

PREPARATION TIME　　　　**COOKING TIME**

2.5kg leg lamb, with shank intact

6 cloves garlic, sliced

6 sprigs thyme,
　　cut into 2cm pieces

2 tablespoons olive oil

4 medium brown onions (600g),
　　chopped coarsely

6 medium tomatoes (900g),
　　peeled, seeded,
　　chopped coarsely

2 bay leaves

⅓ cup (80ml) brandy

2 cups (500ml) dry white wine

8 medium (1.6kg) washed
　　potatoes, peeled, quartered

1 cup (250ml) chicken stock

1　Pierce lamb 12 times with a sharp knife; press one slice of garlic and one piece of thyme into each cut. Reserve remaining garlic and thyme. Rub salt and pepper all over lamb.

2　Preheat oven to moderate.

3　Heat half of the oil in large flameproof baking dish; add lamb, cook until browned all over, remove from dish.

4　Heat remaining oil in same dish; cook onion, reserved garlic and thyme until soft, but not coloured. Add tomato; cook, stirring, until softened. Add bay leaves, brandy and wine; bring to a boil.

5　Return leg of lamb to dish; roast, uncovered, in moderate oven about 30 minutes. Add potatoes to same dish and roast 1 hour and 10 minutes or until lamb is cooked as desired and potato is tender. Spoon pan juices over lamb occasionally during cooking.

6　Remove lamb from dish; cover with foil, stand 15 minutes.

7　Meanwhile, strain the cooking juices into medium saucepan; reserve tomato mixture and cover to keep warm. Skim fat from top of juices in saucepan. Add chicken stock to saucepan; bring to a boil and boil, uncovered, for 5 minutes or until reduced to 1½ cups (375ml).

8　Serve lamb with potato, tomato mixture and sauce.

serves 8

per serving 17.5g fat; 2227kJ (532 cal)

TIP The lamb can be prepared with the garlic and thyme a day ahead.

rack of lamb with tomatoes

PREPARATION TIME   **COOKING TIME**

To "french trim" meat is to remove the excess gristle and fat from the end of a shank, cutlet or rack to expose the bone. Ask your butcher to prepare the lamb racks for this recipe.

¼ cup (60ml) olive oil
2 racks of lamb (6 cutlets each), french trimmed
4 cloves garlic, sliced thinly
12 truss tomatoes on the vine (900g)
1 tablespoon balsamic vinegar
¼ cup loosely packed fresh basil leaves

1 Preheat oven to hot.
2 Heat 1 tablespoon of the oil in flameproof baking dish; add lamb, cook over high heat until browned. Press half the garlic over lamb.
3 Make a small slit in tomato skins. Add tomato to dish with lamb, pour remaining oil over tomato, top with remaining garlic.
4 Roast in hot oven about 15 minutes or until lamb and tomato are cooked as desired. Remove from dish; cover, stand 10 minutes.
5 Add balsamic vinegar to baking dish, stir to combine with pan juices.
6 Slice lamb; serve with tomato and pan juices, sprinkled with basil leaves.

serves 4
per serving 33.7g fat; 1751kJ (418 cal)
TIP This recipe is best made close to serving.

curried lamb and lentil salad

PREPARATION TIME   **COOKING TIME**

1 Combine 1 tablespoon of the curry paste and 1 tablespoon of the oil in small bowl. Rub lamb with curry mixture.

2 Cook lamb on heated oiled grill pan (or pan-fry) until browned on both sides and cooked as desired. Transfer to plate, cover, stand for 5 minutes.

3 Meanwhile, heat remaining oil in medium saucepan; add onion, carrot and celery, cook, stirring, until vegetables are soft. Add garlic and remaining curry paste, cook, stirring, until fragrant. Add stock and lentils, stir until hot. Remove from heat, add spinach and coriander; toss until combined.

4 Slice lamb; serve with lentil salad.

serves 4

per serving 23.1g fat; 1707kJ (408 cal)

TIPS Lamb can be prepared several hours ahead. Recipe best made just before serving.

2 tablespoons mild curry paste
¼ cup (60ml) peanut oil
600g lamb sirloin (or eye of loin or backstrap)
1 medium brown onion (150g), chopped finely
1 large carrot (180g), chopped finely
1 trimmed celery stalk (100g), chopped finely
1 clove garlic, crushed
⅓ cup (80ml) chicken stock
400g can brown lentils, rinsed, drained
100g baby spinach leaves
½ cup loosely packed fresh coriander leaves

curried lamb shanks with naan

PREPARATION TIME ⬩ **COOKING TIME** ⬩

8 french-trimmed
   lamb shanks (1.5kg)
¼ cup (35g) plain flour
2 tablespoons peanut oil
1 medium brown onion (150g),
   chopped finely
2 cloves garlic, crushed
½ cup (150g) rogan josh
   curry paste
2 cups (500ml) water
400g can crushed tomatoes
1 teaspoon sugar
2 cups (500ml) beef stock
400g cauliflower,
   chopped coarsely
400g pumpkin, chopped coarsely
¾ cup (150g) red lentils
¼ cup coarsely chopped
   fresh coriander
4 pieces naan

1 Toss lamb in flour; shake away excess. Heat oil in large saucepan; cook lamb, in batches, until browned all over.
2 Cook onion and garlic in same pan, stirring, until onion softens. Add paste; cook, stirring, until fragrant. Return lamb to pan with the water, undrained tomatoes, sugar and stock; bring to a boil. Reduce heat; simmer, covered, 1½ hours.
3 Preheat oven to hot.
4 Add cauliflower, pumpkin and lentils to curry; bring to a boil. Reduce heat; simmer, covered, 15 minutes or until cooked as desired. Remove from heat; stir in coriander.
5 Meanwhile, wrap naan in foil; heat in hot oven 10 minutes. Serve naan with lamb.

serves 4
per serving 48.1g fat; 4172kJ (998 cal)
TIPS Naan is a leavened indian bread that is traditionally baked by pressing it against the inside wall of a heated tandoor (brick oven).
You can use any type of curry paste from mild tikka to fiery vindaloo, depending on how spicy you want your lamb to be.
Ask your butcher to french trim the lamb shanks for this recipe.

lamb cutlets and salsa verde

PREPARATION TIME | **COOKING TIME**

8 double lamb cutlets (1.2kg),
  french trimmed

SALSA VERDE
½ cup finely chopped fresh
  flat-leaf parsley
¼ cup finely chopped fresh basil
2 tablespoons finely chopped
  fresh mint
4 anchovies, drained,
  chopped finely
1 tablespoon drained capers,
  chopped finely
1 clove garlic, crushed
2 teaspoons dijon mustard
2 tablespoons red wine vinegar
⅓ cup (80ml) extra virgin olive oil

1 Make salsa verde.
2 Cook lamb on preheated grill pan or in heavy-based frying pan until
   browned on both sides and cooked as desired.
3 Slice lamb; serve with salsa verde.
   SALSA VERDE Combine herbs, anchovy, capers, garlic, mustard and
   vinegar in small bowl. Gradually stir in the oil. Cover surface of sauce
   with plastic wrap to prevent discolouration.

serves 4
per serving 44.3g fat; 2192kJ (524 cal)
TIPS Double lamb cutlets can be two cutlets together or two cutlets
with one centre bone.
Salsa verde can be made three hours ahead.

lemon grass lamb in lettuce cups

PREPARATION TIME   **COOKING TIME**

1 Place lettuce in large bowl of iced water; stand 10 minutes. Drain; pat
  dry with absorbent paper.
2 Meanwhile, place vermicelli in large heatproof bowl; cover with boiling
  water. Stand until just tender; drain. Cut carrot into long thin strips.
3 Heat half of the oil in wok or large frying pan; stir-fry lamb, in batches,
  until browned all over. Cover to keep warm.
4 Heat remaining oil in wok; stir-fry carrot until just tender. Add garlic,
  ginger, lemon grass and lime leaves; stir-fry until lemon grass softens.
  Return lamb to wok with vermicelli, juice, sauces and half of the chives;
  stir-fry until heated through.
5 Place two lettuce leaves on each serving plate; divide lamb mixture
  among leaves, sprinkle with remaining chives.

serves 4
per serving 22.5g fat; 1920kJ (459 cal)

8 iceberg lettuce leaves
100g rice vermicelli
1 medium carrot (120g)
2 tablespoons peanut oil
750g lamb strips
4 cloves garlic, crushed
4cm piece fresh ginger (20g),
  sliced thinly
2 tablespoons finely chopped
  fresh lemon grass
2 fresh kaffir lime leaves,
  sliced thinly
1 tablespoon lime juice
¼ cup (60ml) sweet chilli sauce
¼ cup (60ml) fish sauce
¼ cup coarsely chopped
  fresh chives

roast lamb with indian spice paste

PREPARATION TIME 15 MINUTES (PLUS REFRIGERATION TIME) **COOKING TIME** 1 HOUR 30 MINUTES (PLUS STANDING TIME)

1.5kg easy-carve leg of lamb
1 cup (250ml) water

INDIAN SPICE PASTE

2 teaspoons coriander seeds
1 teaspoon cumin seeds
2 cardamom pods, bruised
1 cinnamon stick
1 star anise
1 teaspoon ground turmeric
½ teaspoon chilli powder
1 medium brown onion (150g),
    chopped coarsely
2 cloves garlic, peeled
4cm piece fresh ginger (20g),
    grated finely
1 teaspoon salt
2 teaspoons brown sugar
2 tablespoons lemon juice
⅓ cup (80ml) peanut oil

CORIANDER YOGURT

1 cup (280g) yogurt
¼ cup coarsely chopped
    fresh coriander

1 Make indian spice paste.
2 Using the point of a sharp knife, pierce lamb all over with deep cuts. Place lamb and indian spice paste in a large resealable snap-lock bag or large shallow dish. Rub lamb with indian spice paste to ensure an even coating; cover, refrigerate 3 hours or overnight.
3 Preheat oven to moderate.
4 Pour the water into large baking dish; place lamb on rack in dish. Cover with foil; roast in moderate oven 1 hour. Remove foil, roast, uncovered, 30 minutes or until lamb is browned and cooked as desired. Stand, covered, 15 minutes before slicing.
5 Meanwhile, make coriander yogurt.
6 Serve lamb with coriander yogurt.
INDIAN SPICE PASTE Combine seeds, cardamom, cinnamon and star anise in heated, dry frying pan; cook, stirring, until fragrant. Add turmeric and chilli, remove from heat. Blend or process spices with onion, garlic, ginger, salt, sugar and juice until smooth. While motor is running, gradually add oil until well combined.
CORIANDER YOGURT Combine yogurt and coriander in small bowl.

serves 6
per serving 23.3g fat; 1709kJ (408 cal)
TIP Paste is also suitable for beef, chicken or pork.

garlic and sage lamb racks with roasted red onion

PREPARATION TIME 10 MINUTES **COOKING TIME** 30 MINUTES (PLUS STANDING TIME)

3 large red onions (900g)

⅓ cup (80ml) extra virgin olive oil

2 tablespoons coarsely chopped fresh sage

4 cloves garlic, chopped coarsely

4 racks of lamb (4 cutlets each), french trimmed

1 Preheat oven to hot.

2 Halve onion, slice into thin wedges; place in large baking dish with half of the oil.

3 Combine remaining oil in small bowl with sage and garlic. Press sage mixture all over lamb; place lamb on onion.

4 Roast, uncovered, in hot oven about 25 minutes or until lamb is browned all over and cooked as desired. Cover with foil; stand 10 minutes.

serves 4

per serving 44.2g fat; 2395 kJ (572 cal)

TIP Red onions are sweet and have a less aggressive scent than their brown and white counterparts.

herb and garlic barbecued lamb

PREPARATION TIME   **COOKING TIME**

1 Place lamb in large shallow dish; pour combined oil, garlic, mustard, wine and rosemary over lamb. Cover; refrigerate 3 hours or overnight.
2 Remove lamb from marinade; place marinade in small saucepan, reserve. Place lamb, covered with foil, on heated oiled grill plate (or grill or barbecue); cook about 30 minutes or until cooked as desired, turning halfway through cooking time.
3 Brush lamb all over with jelly; cook, uncovered, until jelly melts and forms a glaze. Stand lamb, covered, 10 minutes before slicing.
4 Meanwhile, add stock to reserved marinade; bring to a boil. Reduce heat; simmer, uncovered, 5 minutes. Serve sliced lamb with sauce.

2kg butterflied leg of lamb
¼ cup (60ml) olive oil
3 cloves garlic, crushed
2 tablespoons wholegrain mustard
¾ cup (180ml) dry white wine
1 tablespoon finely chopped
    fresh rosemary
2 tablespoons mint jelly
¼ cup (60ml) chicken stock

serves 8
per serving 22.3g fat; 1594kJ (381 cal)
TIP Lamb also can be cooked, covered, in hot oven for about 25 minutes or until cooked as desired.

lamb cutlets with olive salsa, polenta and fennel

PREPARATION TIME 10 MINUTES **COOKING TIME** 20 MINUTES

12 lamb cutlets (900g),
    french trimmed
1½ cups (375ml) water
2 cups (500ml) chicken stock
1 cup (170g) instant polenta
⅓ cup (30g) finely grated
    parmesan cheese
½ cup (125ml) cream
2 tablespoons olive oil
4 baby fennel bulbs (600g),
    sliced thinly
1 cup seeded black olives (100g),
    chopped coarsely
2 tablespoons lemon juice
1 clove garlic, crushed
1 tablespoon coarsely chopped
    fresh flat-leaf parsley

1 Cook lamb on heated oiled grill plate (or grill or barbecue) until browned both sides and cooked as desired.

2 Meanwhile, combine the water and stock in medium saucepan; bring to a boil. Stir in polenta gradually; cook, stirring, over low heat until mixture thickens. Stir in cheese and cream.

3 Heat half of the oil in medium frying pan; cook fennel, stirring, until tender.

4 Combine remaining oil with olives, juice, garlic and parsley in small bowl. Serve lamb with polenta, fennel and olive salsa.

serves 4
per serving 41g fat; 2875kJ (687 cal)

pork and black bean stir-fry

PREPARATION TIME 25 MINUTES (PLUS REFRIGERATION TIME) **COOKING TIME** 25 MINUTES

1 small fresh red thai chilli,
  seeded, chopped finely
1 clove garlic, crushed
¾ cup (180ml) chicken stock
⅓ cup (80ml) black bean sauce
1 tablespoon oyster sauce
1 teaspoon sesame oil
750g pork fillet, sliced thinly
1 tablespoon peanut oil
1 large brown onion (200g),
  sliced thinly
2 small carrots (140g),
  sliced thinly
2 baby bok choy (300g), trimmed,
  quartered lengthways
425g can baby corn, drained

1 Combine chilli, garlic, stock, sauces, sesame oil and pork in large bowl; toss to coat pork all over in marinade. Cover; refrigerate 3 hours or overnight.

2 Drain pork; reserve marinade. Heat half of the peanut oil in wok or large frying pan; stir-fry pork, in batches, until browned all over.

3 Heat remaining peanut oil in wok; stir-fry onion and carrot until onion just softens. Add bok choy; stir-fry until bok choy is just tender. Return pork to wok with corn; stir-fry until pork is cooked through. Add reserved marinade; bring to a boil. Toss gently to combine.

4 Serve stir-fry on steamed white rice, if desired.

serves 4
per serving 11.7g fat; 1587kJ (380 cal)
TIP You can vary the vegetables if you like, but remember to stir-fry those that take the longest to cook, such as onion, carrot, celery and cauliflower, before faster-cooking vegetables such as mushrooms, capsicum, broccoli or snow peas. Add last those vegetables that need the least cooking time or are the softest, such as cabbage, asian greens, fresh herbs, green onion or bean sprouts.

sticky pork and hokkien noodle stir-fry

PREPARATION TIME 15 MINUTES **COOKING TIME** 10 MINUTES

500g hokkien noodles

2 medium carrots (240g)

2 tablespoons peanut oil

1 medium brown onion (150g),
   sliced thickly

2 cloves garlic, crushed

300g broccoli, chopped coarsely

200g fresh baby corn,
   halved lengthways

600g pork strips

1 teaspoon cornflour

1 tablespoon brown sugar

⅓ cup (80ml) sweet chilli sauce

2 tablespoons kecap manis

1 Place noodles in large heatproof bowl; cover with boiling water. Separate noodles with fork; drain.

2 Cut carrot into thin strips.

3 Heat half of the oil in wok or large frying pan; stir-fry onion and garlic until onion softens. Add carrot, broccoli and corn; stir-fry until just tender. Remove from wok.

4 Heat remaining oil in wok; stir-fry pork, in batches, until browned all over.

5 Blend cornflour and sugar with sauces in small jug. Return vegetables to wok with pork and sauce mixture; stir-fry until sauce boils and thickens slightly. Add noodles; stir-fry until heated through.

serves 4
per serving 21.6g fat; 2519kJ (603 cal)

pork and corn salsa tortilla wraps

PREPARATION TIME   **COOKING TIME**

1 Combine pork, oil and seasoning mix in medium bowl; toss to coat pork.
2 Warm tortillas according to packet directions. Make corn salsa.
3 Cook pork on heated oiled grill plate or large frying pan until pork is browned and tender.
4 Serve pork wrapped in tortillas with corn salsa, lettuce and sour cream.

CORN SALSA Combine corn, tomato, onion and coriander in medium bowl.

serves 4
per serving 20.4g fat; 2279kJ (545 cal)
TIP This recipe can be prepared several hours ahead; cook and assemble just before serving.

600g pork fillet, sliced thinly
2 tablespoons peanut oil
35g packet taco seasoning mix
16 soft corn tortillas
1 butter lettuce, torn
½ cup (120g) light sour cream

CORN SALSA

310g can corn kernels, drained
3 medium tomatoes (450g), chopped coarsely
1 small red onion (100g), chopped finely
½ cup coarsely chopped fresh coriander

honey soy pork with spinach and snow pea salad

You need approximately 3 limes
for this recipe.

1.6kg pork neck
4 cloves garlic, crushed
¼ cup (60ml) olive oil
2 tablespoons brown sugar
⅓ cup (120g) honey
4cm piece fresh ginger (20g),
 grated finely
¼ cup (60ml) light soy sauce
¼ cup (60ml) lime juice

SPINACH AND
 SNOW PEA SALAD
200g baby spinach leaves
100g snow peas, trimmed,
 sliced thinly
4 green onions, sliced thinly
⅓ cup (50g) toasted pine nuts,
 chopped coarsely
½ cup (40g) flaked parmesan
 cheese
⅓ cup (80ml) olive oil
1 teaspoon finely grated lime rind
¼ cup (60ml) lime juice
1 tablespoon sugar

1 Place pork in large shallow dish; pour combined remaining
 ingredients over pork. Cover; refrigerate 3 hours or overnight,
 turning pork occasionally in marinade.
2 Preheat oven to moderate.
3 Drain pork; reserve marinade. Wrap pork in three layers of foil,
 securing ends tightly. Roast in moderate oven about 2 hours
 or until cooked as desired. Stand 10 minutes; slice thinly.
4 Meanwhile, place reserved marinade in small saucepan; bring to
 a boil. Reduce heat; simmer, uncovered, 5 minutes. Drizzle pork
 with marinade; accompany with spinach and snow pea salad.
 SPINACH AND SNOW PEA SALAD Place spinach, snow peas,
 onion, nuts and cheese in large bowl. Just before serving, add
 combined remaining ingredients; toss gently to combine.

serves 8
per serving 31.3g fat; 2264kJ (542 cal)

singapore noodles

PREPARATION TIME 15 MINUTES **COOKING TIME** 10 MINUTES

250g dried thin egg noodles

2 tablespoons peanut oil

4 eggs, beaten lightly

1 tablespoon water

1 medium brown onion (150g),
  chopped finely

2 cloves garlic, crushed

2 tablespoons mild curry paste

200g pork mince

200g chinese barbecued pork,
  sliced thinly

200g cooked shelled small prawns

3 green onions, chopped coarsely

¼ cup (60ml) salt-reduced
  soy sauce

2 tablespoons oyster sauce

2 small fresh red thai chillies,
  seeded, chopped finely

1 Cook noodles in large saucepan of boiling water, uncovered, until just tender; drain.

2 Meanwhile, heat 2 teaspoons of the oil in wok or large frying pan; add half of the combined eggs and water, swirl wok to make thin omelette. Cook, uncovered, until egg is just set. Remove from wok; roll omelette, cut into thin strips. Heat another 2 teaspoons of the oil in wok; repeat process with remaining egg mixture.

3 Heat remaining oil in wok; stir-fry brown onion and garlic until onion softens. Add paste; stir-fry until fragrant. Add pork mince; stir-fry until changed in colour. Add barbecued pork, prawns, green onion, sauces, chilli and half of the omelette; stir-fry until heated through. Add noodles; toss gently to combine, serve topped with remaining omelette.

serves 4
per serving 24.5g fat; 2683kJ (642 cal)

oven-baked risotto with italian sausages

PREPARATION TIME   **COOKING TIME**

1 Preheat oven to moderate.
2 Heat flameproof dish on stove top; add sausages and cook until browned all over and cooked through. Remove from dish; slice thickly.
3 Meanwhile, add stock to medium saucepan; bring to a boil.
4 Heat oil and butter in same flameproof dish; cook onion and garlic, stirring, until soft. Add rice; stir to coat in the onion mixture. Add wine, bring to a boil then simmer, uncovered, 1 minute. Add stock, sausages and tomatoes; cover with lid and cook in moderate oven about 25 minutes or until liquid is absorbed and rice is tender. Stir once during cooking.
5 Stir in the basil and cheese.

serves 6
per serving 33.9g fat; 2855kJ (682 cal)
TIP Recipe is best made close to serving.

500g spicy Italian-style sausages
1 litre (4 cups) chicken stock
1 tablespoon olive oil
40g butter
2 large brown onions (400g), chopped coarsely
1 clove garlic, crushed
2 cups (400g) arborio rice
¾ cup (180ml) dry white wine
1 cup (160g) drained semi-dried tomatoes
¼ cup fresh basil leaves
¼ cup (20g) coarsely grated parmesan cheese

pork loin with fresh peach chutney

PREPARATION TIME 15 MINUTES **COOKING TIME** 3 HOURS

2kg boned pork loin

1 tablespoon olive oil

½ teaspoon celery seeds

1 teaspoon sea salt

FRESH PEACH CHUTNEY

2 large peaches (440g),
  chopped coarsely

1 large brown onion (200g),
  chopped coarsely

¼ cup (40g) coarsely
  chopped raisins

2cm piece fresh ginger (10g),
  grated finely

1 cup (220g) sugar

1 cup (250ml) apple cider vinegar

1 cinnamon stick

¼ teaspoon ground clove

1. Make fresh peach chutney.
2. Preheat oven to hot.
3. Remove rind from loin; reserve. Rub pork with half of the oil; sprinkle with seeds.
4. Place pork on wire rack in large baking dish; roast, uncovered, in hot oven, about 1 hour or until juices run clear when pierced with skewer. Remove from oven; place pork on board, cover to keep warm.
5. Increase oven temperature to very hot.
6. Remove excess fat from underside of reserved rind; score rind, rub with remaining oil and sea salt. Place rind, fatty-side up, on wire rack in baking dish; roast, uncovered, in very hot oven about 15 minutes or until crisp and browned. Drain on absorbent paper.
7. Serve thickly sliced pork and rind with peach chutney. Accompany with a fresh salad of your choice.

FRESH PEACH CHUTNEY Combine ingredients in medium saucepan, stir over heat, without boiling, until sugar dissolves. Bring to a boil, reduce heat; simmer, uncovered, stirring occasionally, about 1¾ hours or until mixture thickens.

serves 6
per serving 15.9g fat; 2605kJ (623 cal)
TIP The chutney can be made up to a week ahead. Place in a sterilised jar while still hot; seal, cool, then refrigerate until required.

capsicum and pancetta with cellentani

PREPARATION TIME   **COOKING TIME**

500g cellentani or curly pasta
¼ cup (60ml) extra virgin olive oil
150g sliced pancetta,
   chopped coarsely
3 cloves garlic, crushed
3 medium tomatoes (450g),
   peeled, seeded,
   chopped coarsely
300g roasted red capsicum,
   sliced thinly
1 cup firmly packed fresh
   flat-leaf parsley leaves
1 tablespoon baby capers,
   rinsed, drained

1 Cook pasta in large saucepan of boiling water, uncovered, until just tender; drain.
2 Meanwhile, heat 1 tablespoon of the oil in large frying pan, add pancetta, cook, stirring, until crisp; remove from pan. Add garlic, tomato and capsicum to pan; cook, stirring, until softened. Remove from heat and stir in parsley and capers.
3 Combine pasta with tomato mixture, pancetta, remaining oil and pepper to taste; toss gently.

serves 6
per serving 13.6g fat; 1801kJ (432 cal)
TIP Recipe is best made close to serving.

roasted pumpkin, bacon and fetta frittata

PREPARATION TIME　　　　**COOKING TIME**

1　Preheat oven to hot.
2　Combine pumpkin and oil in large baking dish; roast, uncovered, in hot oven 15 minutes. Add onion, bacon and garlic; roast, uncovered, about 15 minutes or until pumpkin and bacon are browned lightly.
3　Meanwhile, grease deep 19cm-square cake pan; sprinkle base and sides with half of the parmesan.
4　Reduce oven temperature to moderate. Spoon pumpkin mixture into prepared pan. Whisk eggs in medium bowl with remaining parmesan and blended cornflour and cream. Pour egg mixture over pumpkin mixture; sprinkle with fetta.
5　Bake, uncovered, in moderate oven about 45 minutes or until frittata sets. Stand 10 minutes; turn out. Cut into quarters; serve with a fresh green salad, if desired.

600g pumpkin, chopped coarsely
1 tablespoon olive oil
6 green onions, cut into 5cm pieces
4 bacon rashers, rind removed, chopped coarsely
1 clove garlic, crushed
½ cup (40g) finely grated parmesan cheese
6 eggs
2 teaspoons cornflour
½ cup (125ml) cream
100g fetta cheese, crumbled

serves 4
per serving 38.4g fat; 2099kJ (502 cal)

glazed pork and veal apple meatloaf

PREPARATION TIME   **COOKING TIME**

2 teaspoons olive oil

1 small brown onion (80g), chopped finely

2 cloves garlic, sliced thinly

1 trimmed celery stalk (100g), chopped finely

1 medium green apple (150g), peeled, grated coarsely

500g pork and veal mince mixture

1 cup (70g) stale breadcrumbs

1 tablespoon coarsely chopped fresh sage

1 egg, beaten lightly

10 thin streaky bacon rashers

1 small green apple (130g), cored, sliced thinly, extra

2 tablespoons apple jelly (or redcurrant or quince jelly)

1 Heat oil in large frying pan; add onion, garlic and celery; cook, stirring, until onion is soft. Add apple and cook, stirring, until all the liquid has evaporated; cool.

2 Preheat oven to moderate.

3 In large bowl, combine onion mixture with the mince, breadcrumbs, sage and egg; mix well.

4 Transfer mince mixture to large sheet of plastic wrap; use wrap to roll mixture into 8cm x 24cm log, discard wrap. Wrap bacon around log, alternating extra apple slices with bacon.

5 Place meatloaf onto an oiled oven tray, brush all over with half the warmed jelly. Roast, uncovered, in moderate oven about 45 minutes, brushing halfway through cooking with remaining jelly, or until meatloaf is cooked through and bacon is browned and crisp. Serve with mustard, if desired.

serves 4

per serving 17.5g fat; 1988kJ (475 cal)

pork ribs with honey sesame marinade

PREPARATION TIME   **COOKING TIME**

1 Make honey sesame marinade.
2 Pour two-thirds of the marinade into a large shallow dish or large resealable bag. Add pork spare ribs, cover, refrigerate 3 hours or overnight, turning occasionally.
3 Preheat oven to moderately slow.
4 Drain ribs from marinade, discard marinade. Line two baking dishes with baking paper or foil (this prevents honey mixture from burning onto baking dishes). Place a wire rack in each dish. Place pork ribs in a single layer on racks. Roast, uncovered, about 45 minutes, turning halfway and brushing with remaining marinade, until well browned and cooked through.
5 Cut racks into individual ribs before serving.
   HONEY SESAME MARINADE Combine ingredients in small bowl.

serves 6
per serving 11g fat; 2512kJ (600 cal)
TIPS Marinade also suitable for poultry.
Ribs are best roasted just before serving.

4 racks American-style
  pork spare ribs (1.5kg)

HONEY SESAME MARINADE
¼ cup (90g) honey
½ cup (125ml) kecap manis
2 teaspoons sesame oil
2 star anise
1 tablespoon sesame seeds,
  toasted
3cm piece fresh ginger (15g),
  grated finely
1 clove garlic, crushed

roast chicken and beetroot with pesto butter

PREPARATION TIME   **COOKING TIME**

1.6kg chicken
1 medium white onion (150g),
   quartered
1 bulb garlic, cloves separated
cooking-oil spray
1 teaspoon salt
8 small fresh beetroot (1kg),
   trimmed

PESTO BUTTER

125g butter, softened
1 tablespoon lemon juice
⅓ cup coarsely chopped
   fresh basil
2 tablespoons pine nuts, toasted
2 cloves garlic, crushed
2 tablespoons grated
   parmesan cheese

1 Make pesto butter.
2 Preheat oven to moderate.
3 Wash the cavity of the chicken under cold water; pat dry with absorbent
   paper. Tuck wings under chicken. Loosen skin of chicken by sliding
   fingers carefully between skin and meat. Spread half the pesto butter
   under the skin; spread mixture evenly over breast by pressing with fingers.
   Place onion and two of the garlic cloves inside chicken cavity. Tie legs
   of chicken together using kitchen string.
4 Place chicken, breast side up, on wire rack in large baking dish. Spray
   chicken all over with cooking spray; sprinkle with salt. Roast, uncovered,
   in moderate oven 45 minutes.
5 Add unpeeled beetroot to dish; roast, uncovered, 15 minutes. Add
   remaining unpeeled garlic cloves to dish; roast about 30 minutes or
   until chicken and beetroot are cooked when tested. Cover loosely with
   foil if chicken starts to over-brown.
6 Cover chicken to keep warm; stand 10 minutes. Meanwhile, peel beetroot.
7 Serve chicken with beetroot, garlic and remaining pesto butter.
   PESTO BUTTER Blend or process ingredients until almost smooth.

serves 4
per serving 65.5g fat; 3621kJ (865 cal)
TIPS Pesto butter can be made a day ahead.
Recipe best made close to serving.

tandoori chicken salad with pappadums

PREPARATION TIME   **COOKING TIME**

Pappadums of many different flavours are available ready to cook. They taste great deep-fried, but for a low-fat version, we "puffed" the pappadums in a microwave oven.

8 chicken tenderloins (600g)
¼ cup (100g) tandoori paste
1½ cups (400g) yogurt
12 pappadums
¼ cup (60ml) mint sauce
250g mesclun
4 large egg tomatoes (360g), chopped coarsely
2 lebanese cucumbers (260g), halved lengthways, sliced thickly

1 Combine chicken with paste and half the yogurt in medium bowl; toss to coat chicken all over. Cook chicken, in batches, on heated oiled grill plate (or grill or barbecue) until browned all over and cooked through.

2 Meanwhile, place four pappadums around edge of microwave-safe plate; cook on HIGH (100%) about 30 seconds or until puffed. Repeat with remaining pappadums.

3 Combine remaining yogurt in small bowl with sauce. Divide mesclun among serving plates; top with tomato, cucumber, chicken and yogurt mint sauce. Accompany salad with pappadums.

serves 4
per serving 20.2g fat; 1878kJ (449 cal)
TIP Lamb fillets make a great variation to this recipe.

honey ginger baked chicken

PREPARATION TIME

COOKING TIME

1 Peel ginger; slice thinly. Stack slices; slice crossways thinly to create strips. Remove rind thinly from lemon using a zester, or peel rind with a vegetable peeler, avoiding the white pith; cut rind into thin strips.

2 Combine the water, honey and sugar in medium saucepan over medium heat; cook, stirring, until sugar is dissolved. Bring to a boil; add ginger, then simmer, stirring, for 5 minutes or until ginger is tender.

3 Transfer ginger mixture to large heatproof bowl. Add garlic, chilli and rind; stir to combine. Cut deep slashes at 2cm intervals through thickest part of chicken flesh. Place chicken in ginger mixture and turn to coat evenly. Cover; refrigerate 3 hours or overnight, turning chicken occasionally.

4 Preheat oven to moderate.

5 Place chicken mixture in single layer in medium baking dish. Bake chicken, uncovered, in moderate oven about 40 minutes or until chicken is cooked through and browned.

6 Serve chicken topped with green onions, and steamed white rice, if desired.

10cm piece fresh ginger (50g)
1 medium lemon (140g)
¼ cup (60ml) water
⅓ cup (120g) honey
¼ cup (55g) brown sugar
2 cloves garlic, crushed
1 large green chilli, seeded, chopped (optional)
4 chicken thigh cutlets (640g)
4 chicken drumsticks (600g)
3 green onions, sliced thinly

serves 4

per serving 19g fat; 2012kJ (481 cal)

TIP Chicken best marinated a day ahead.

mediterranean chicken salad

PREPARATION TIME   **COOKING TIME**

1½ cups (375ml) chicken stock
½ cup (125ml) dry white wine
4 single chicken breast fillets (680g)
2 medium yellow capsicums (400g)
1 large loaf sourdough bread (500g)
100g butter, melted
2 cloves garlic, crushed
1 tablespoon finely chopped
   fresh flat-leaf parsley
150g baby rocket leaves
250g teardrop tomatoes, halved
⅓ cup (40g) seeded black olives

ANCHOVY DRESSING
½ cup firmly packed fresh
   basil leaves
½ cup (125ml) extra virgin olive oil
2 tablespoons finely grated
   parmesan cheese
2 anchovy fillets, drained
1 tablespoon lemon juice

1 Bring stock and wine to a boil in large frying pan. Add chicken, reduce heat; simmer, covered, about 8 minutes or until cooked through, turning once halfway through cooking time. Stand chicken in stock for 10 minutes; slice chicken thinly, reserve stock for another use, if desired.

2 Meanwhile, quarter capsicums; remove and discard seeds and membranes. Roast under grill, skin-side up, until skin blisters and blackens. Cover capsicum pieces with plastic wrap or paper for 5 minutes. Peel away skin; slice capsicum thinly.

3 Preheat oven to moderately hot.

4 Cut bread into 1.5cm slices; remove and discard crusts, cut slices into 3cm cubes. Toss bread in large bowl with combined butter, garlic and parsley; spread bread, in single layer, over two oven trays. Toast, uncovered, in moderately hot oven about 10 minutes or until croutons are crisp and lightly browned.

5 Make anchovy dressing.

6 Place chicken, capsicum and croutons in large bowl with rocket, tomato and olives, add anchovy dressing; toss gently to combine.
ANCHOVY DRESSING Blend or process ingredients until smooth.

serves 4
per serving 61.7g fat; 3787kJ (906 cal)
TIP Chicken can be poached and croutons toasted the day ahead. Store croutons in an airtight container. Refrigerate chicken, covered, until ready to assemble salad.

chicken pitta pockets

PREPARATION TIME   **COOKING TIME**

8 chicken tenderloins (600g)

2 teaspoons Seasoned Salt

1 medium brown onion (150g),
  sliced thinly

4 pocket pitta

4 large green oak leaf lettuce
  leaves, torn

8 pieces sliced pickled cucumber,
  drained

2 small egg tomatoes (120g),
  sliced thinly

¼ cup (75g) low-fat mayonnaise

2 teaspoons water

2 teaspoons wholegrain mustard

1 Combine chicken and salt in large bowl; toss to coat chicken all over.
2 Heat large oiled non-stick frying pan; cook onion, stirring, until just softened, remove from pan. Cook chicken, in batches, until browned all over and cooked through.
3 Cut each pitta in half through centre; open out each half to form pockets. Divide chicken, onion, lettuce, cucumber and tomato among pitta pockets; drizzle with combined remaining ingredients.

serves 4
per serving 8g fat; 2084kJ (498 cal)
TIPS Pitta, a middle-eastern flat bread made from white or wholemeal flour, can be eaten whole, used as a wrapper or cut into wedges and used as an accompaniment to dips.
"Seasoned Salt" is a tradename for a packaged blend of salt, onion, capsicum, pepper, garlic and celery seed.

warm duck and rice noodle salad

PREPARATION TIME   **COOKING TIME**

1 Place noodles in large heatproof bowl, cover with boiling water, stand until just tender; drain.

2 Discard skin and bones from warm duck; slice meat thinly.

3 Combine juice, sauces and sugar in screw-top jar; shake dressing well.

4 Combine noodles and half of the duck in large bowl with carrot, onion, cabbage, herbs and half of the dressing; toss gently to combine.

5 Serve salad topped with remaining duck, remaining dressing and nuts.

serves 4

per serving 43.8g fat; 2745kJ (657 cal)

TIPS Whole barbecued ducks are available from Asian barbecue shops. You can buy the duck a day ahead, if necessary, and just reheat it in a moderate oven for about 15 minutes before using. Italian sweet basil can be substituted for thai basil.

You will need to purchase approximately half a small chinese cabbage for this recipe.

150g dried rice stick noodles

1kg chinese barbecued duck

¼ cup (60ml) lime juice

2 tablespoons sweet chilli sauce

2 teaspoons fish sauce

1 tablespoon sugar

1 large carrot (180g), sliced thinly

2 green onions, sliced thinly

2 cups (160g) finely shredded
  chinese cabbage

¼ cup loosely packed fresh
  mint leaves

¼ cup loosely packed fresh
  coriander leaves

¼ cup loosely packed fresh
  thai basil leaves

⅓ cup (50g) toasted unsalted
  peanuts, chopped coarsely

thai-style steamed chicken with noodles

PREPARATION TIME **COOKING TIME**

4 large silverbeet leaves

4 single chicken breast fillets (680g)

2 kaffir lime leaves, shredded finely

2 small fresh red thai chillies,
   seeded, sliced thinly

1 tablespoon finely chopped
   lemon grass

500g fresh rice noodles

SWEET CHILLI DRESSING

¼ cup (60ml) sweet chilli sauce

2 teaspoons fish sauce

1 tablespoon lime juice

1 clove garlic, crushed

2 tablespoons finely chopped
   fresh coriander

1 Drop silverbeet into pan of boiling water, drain immediately, then
   dip into bowl of iced water until cold; drain well.

2 Place a chicken fillet on a silverbeet leaf, sprinkle with lime leaves,
   chilli and lemon grass. Wrap silverbeet around chicken to enclose.

3 Line a bamboo steamer with baking paper or a heatproof plate. Place
   chicken in prepared steamer over wok or pan of simmering water.
   Cover and steam about 15 minutes or until cooked through.

4 Meanwhile, place noodles in large heatproof bowl, cover with hot
   water and stand for 5 minutes; drain. Make sweet chilli dressing.

5 Toss half of the sweet chilli dressing through noodles. Serve sliced
   chicken with noodles and remaining sweet chilli dressing.
   SWEET CHILLI DRESSING Combine ingredients in small bowl.

serves 4

per serving 10.4g fat; 1534kJ (367 cal)

TIPS If the silverbeet leaves are small, use two per chicken breast.
If kaffir lime leaves are unavailable, use 2 teaspoons of finely grated
lime rind.

chicken and oyster sauce noodle stir-fry

PREPARATION TIME　　　　　**COOKING TIME**

375g dried rice stick noodles
1 tablespoon sesame oil
1 tablespoon peanut oil
600g chicken thigh fillets, sliced
350g asparagus, chopped coarsely
375g fresh baby corn, halved
2 cloves garlic, crushed
1 cup (250ml) oyster sauce
½ cup chopped fresh garlic chives

1 Add noodles to large saucepan of boiling water. Boil, uncovered, until just tender; drain. Cover to keep warm.
2 Add half the combined oils to heated wok or large frying pan; stir-fry chicken, in batches, until browned and cooked through.
3 Heat remaining oil in wok; stir-fry asparagus, corn and garlic until tender. Return chicken to wok with noodles and oyster sauce; stir-fry until heated through. Stir in chives.

serves 4
per serving 22.2g fat; 2337kJ (558 cal)
　　　Recipe is best made close to serving.

peri peri chicken

PREPARATION TIME   **COOKING TIME**

1 Combine juice, oil, chilli, sugar, paprika, garlic, rosemary and salt in large bowl or resealable plastic bag. Add chicken, coat in marinade. Cover, refrigerate for 3 hours or overnight.

2 Drain chicken from marinade; reserve marinade. Make deep diagonal cuts in chicken pieces.

3 Heat covered barbecue according to manufacturer's instructions. Cook chicken on oiled barbecue by indirect heat, covered, about 25 minutes or until browned on both sides and just cooked through. Brush with reserved marinade frequently during cooking.

⅓ cup (80ml) lemon juice
¼ cup (60ml) olive oil
6 small fresh red thai chillies, seeded, chopped finely
2 teaspoons brown sugar
1 teaspoon sweet paprika
2 cloves garlic, crushed
2 teaspoons finely chopped fresh rosemary
2 teaspoons sea salt
4 chicken maryland pieces (1.4kg)

serves 4
per serving 46.3g fat; 2480kJ (592 cal)
TIP Chicken is best marinated a day ahead.

crisp-skinned soy chicken with spiced salt

PREPARATION TIME   **COOKING TIME**

4 litres (16 cups) water

1 cup (250ml) light soy sauce

5cm piece fresh ginger (25g),
    peeled, sliced thickly

2 cloves garlic, crushed

2 teaspoons five-spice powder

1.5kg chicken

vegetable oil, for deep-frying

SOY MARINADE

1 tablespoon honey

1 tablespoon light soy sauce

1 tablespoon dry sherry

½ teaspoon five-spice powder

½ teaspoon sesame oil

SPICED SALT

¼ cup sea salt

½ teaspoon cracked black pepper

1 teaspoon five-spice powder

1 Combine the water, sauce, ginger, garlic and five-spice in large saucepan; bring to a boil. Boil, uncovered, 2 minutes. Add chicken; return to a boil. Reduce heat; simmer, uncovered, about 10 minutes, turning once during cooking. Remove from heat, cover; stand 30 minutes. Remove chicken from stock; pat dry with absorbent paper.

2 Using kitchen scissors, cut chicken in half through breastbone and along side of backbone; cut legs and wings from chicken halves. Place chicken pieces on tray; coat skin in soy marinade. Cover; refrigerate 2 hours.

3 Heat oil in wok or large, deep frying pan; deep-fry chicken, in batches, until browned all over, drain on absorbent paper.

4 Cut chicken into serving-sized pieces; serve with spiced salt.

SOY MARINADE Combine ingredients in small bowl.

SPICED SALT Heat small non-stick frying pan; cook salt and pepper, stirring, 2 minutes. Add five-spice; cook, stirring, about 1 minute or until fragrant.

serves 4

per serving 41.8g fat; 2300kJ (550 cal)

TIPS When deep-frying, have the pan no more than one-third filled with oil. The stock can be used as a base for an Asian-style soup; refrigerate until cold, then discard fat from the top before using.

barbecued chicken with nam jim

PREPARATION TIME   **COOKING TIME**

1 Cut two deep slashes through the skin and flesh of each chicken thigh. Rub chicken with combined sugar, cumin and salt. Stand 10 minutes.
2 Meanwhile, make nam jim.
3 Place chicken, skin-side down, on lightly oiled, heated grill plate (or on a grill or covered barbecue) on low heat about 10 minutes. Turn, cover with foil or cover the barbecue; cook until chicken is cooked through.
4 Serve chicken on a bed of herbs with nam jim.
   NAM JIM Blend or process ingredients until smooth.

serves 4
per serving 50.2g fat; 3393kJ (810 cal)
TIPS The nam jim can be made up to two hours ahead. Chicken can be prepared several hours ahead.

12 chicken thigh cutlets (2kg)
⅓ cup (90g) grated palm sugar
2 teaspoons ground cumin
1 teaspoon salt
1 cup loosely packed fresh
   mint leaves
1 cup loosely packed fresh
   thai basil leaves

2 cloves garlic, crushed
3 large green chillies, seeded,
   chopped coarsely
2 coriander roots
2 tablespoons fish sauce
2 tablespoons grated palm sugar
3 shallots (75g), chopped coarsely
¼ cup (60ml) lime juice

steamed mussels with saffron, chilli and coriander

PREPARATION TIME

COOKING TIME

¾ cup (180ml) dry white wine
¼ teaspoon saffron strands
1 tablespoon fish sauce
2 teaspoons finely grated lime rind
2.2kg medium black mussels
1 tablespoon peanut oil
4cm piece fresh ginger (20g),
  grated coarsely
2 cloves garlic, crushed
3 small fresh red thai chillies,
  seeded, sliced thinly
2 cups loosely packed fresh
  coriander leaves

1 Heat wine in small saucepan until hot. Add saffron, sauce and rind; remove from heat, stand, covered, about 20 minutes.
2 Meanwhile, scrub mussels and pull away the beards.
3 Heat oil in large saucepan, add ginger, garlic and chilli; cook, stirring, until fragrant. Add wine mixture and mussels; simmer, covered, about 5 minutes or until mussels open. Discard any mussels that don't open. Stir in half of the coriander.
4 Spoon mussels and broth into large serving bowls; sprinkle with remaining coriander.

serves 4
per serving 6.6g fat; 720kJ (172 cal)
TIP Recipe is best made close to serving.

ginger and chilli baked fish

PREPARATION TIME　　　　**COOKING TIME**

1.6kg whole white fish

cooking oil spray

2 limes, sliced thinly

2cm piece fresh ginger (10g),
　sliced thinly

1 tablespoon peanut oil

1 tablespoon fish sauce

8cm piece fresh ginger (40g),
　grated finely, extra

1 clove garlic, crushed

2 tablespoons grated palm sugar

1 large fresh red chilli, sliced

1 tablespoon fish sauce, extra

1 tablespoon lime juice

1　Preheat oven to hot.

2　Make four deep slits diagonally across both sides of fish. Place a large sheet of foil, with sides overlapping, in large, shallow baking dish. Spray foil with oil, place fish on foil. Fill fish cavity with layers of lime and ginger.

3　Combine oil, sauce, extra ginger and garlic in small bowl; rub into cuts in fish and all over surface. Bring foil up around sides of fish to catch cooking juices; do not cover top. Bake in hot oven about 20 minutes or until almost cooked through.

4　Meanwhile, combine sugar, chilli, extra sauce and juice in small bowl; spoon over fish. Bake 5 minutes or until fish is browned and just cooked through.

serves 4

per serving　11.4g fat; 1335kJ (319 cal)

TIPS　Fish can be rubbed with ginger mixture six hours ahead. Fish is best cooked just before serving.

salmon with herb and walnut crust

PREPARATION TIME   **COOKING TIME**

1 Preheat oven to moderately hot.
2 Place fish in large baking dish, brush with oil. Roast, uncovered, 5 minutes.
3 Meanwhile, combine remaining ingredients in a medium bowl.
4 Remove fish from oven, sprinkle with three-quarters of parsley mixture. Roast fish 5 minutes. Fish will be rare in the thicker end of the fillet. You can adjust cooking time to suit your taste.
5 Transfer fish to serving platter; sprinkle with the remaining parsley mixture. Serve with lemon wedges, if desired.

serves 6
per serving 21.3g fat; 1365kJ (326 cal)
TIPS Parsley mixture can be made several hours ahead.
Salmon can be cooked several hours ahead and served cold, if preferred, otherwise, roast close to serving.

1kg piece salmon fillet
1 tablespoon olive oil
½ cup coarsely chopped fresh
   flat-leaf parsley
¼ cup coarsely chopped fresh dill
1 clove garlic, crushed
2 teaspoons finely grated
   lemon rind
¼ cup (30g) coarsely chopped
   toasted walnuts
2 teaspoons lemon juice
1 tablespoon olive oil, extra

seafood thai green curry

PREPARATION TIME   **COOKING TIME**

300g black mussels
200g firm white fish fillet
500g medium green prawns
200g scallops with roe
1 tablespoon peanut oil
¼ cup green curry paste
400ml coconut milk
3 finger eggplants (200g),
    sliced finely
½ cup whole fresh
    thai basil leaves
1 tablespoon lime juice
1 tablespoon fish sauce
⅓ cup firmly packed fresh
    coriander leaves

GREEN CURRY PASTE

½ teaspoon ground cumin
1 teaspoon ground coriander
1 teaspoon freshly ground
    black pepper
1 teaspoon ground turmeric
2 cloves garlic, quartered
6 red shallots, quartered
2 sticks lemon grass, trimmed,
    sliced thinly
15 long green chillies, sliced thinly
2cm piece fresh ginger (10g),
    grated coarsely
¼ cup coarsely chopped
    coriander roots and stems
2 kaffir lime leaves, sliced thinly
2 tablespoons peanut oil
1 tablespoon water
1 teaspoon shrimp paste

1   Make green curry paste.
2   Remove beards from mussels and scrub thoroughly. Cut fish into
    5cm squares. Peel and devein prawns. Devein scallops if necessary.
3   Heat oil in large frying pan or saucepan; add curry paste, cook, stirring,
    until fragrant.
4   Add coconut milk; bring to a boil. Reduce heat, simmer, uncovered,
    about 15 minutes or until oil separates from coconut milk. Add eggplant,
    basil, juice and sauce; simmer, uncovered, until eggplant is tender.
5   Add seafood, cook, covered, about 3 minutes or until seafood is just
    cooked through. Discard any mussels that do not open.
6   Stir in coriander. Serve with steamed jasmine rice, if desired.
    GREEN CURRY PASTE Combine cumin, coriander, pepper and
    turmeric in small dry frying pan; cook, stirring, about 2 minutes or
    until fragrant. Blend or process spices with all remaining ingredients
    until a smooth paste is formed. Makes about 1½ cups.

serves 4
per serving 42.8g fat; 2362kJ (564 cal)
TIPS Keep remaining green curry in a glass jar in the refrigerator for
up to four weeks, or freeze in an airtight container.
We used ling for the fish in this recipe. The combination of seafood
can vary according to availability.

prawn and green onion skewers

PREPARATION TIME   **COOKING TIME**

1.5kg medium uncooked prawns
2 tablespoons lime juice
1 tablespoon olive oil
2 cloves garlic, crushed
12 green onions

1 Shell and devein prawns, leaving tails intact. Combine prawns in medium bowl with juice, oil and garlic. Cover; refrigerate 1 hour.
2 Cut onions into 4cm lengths. Thread prawns and onion onto skewers. Cook on heated oiled grill plate (or grill or barbecue) until prawns change colour.

serves 4
per serving 6g fat; 920kJ (220 cal)
TIP Soak 12 bamboo skewers in water for at least 1 hour prior to use, to prevent them from scorching and splintering. If using metal skewers, oil them first to stop the prawns from sticking.

chilli and garlic octopus

PREPARATION TIME   **COOKING TIME**

1 Cook seeds in small dry frying pan, stirring, about 1 minute or until fragrant. Place seeds in large bowl with octopus, oil, garlic, juice and sauce; toss to combine. Cover; refrigerate 3 hours or overnight.
2 Cook drained octopus on heated oiled grill plate (or grill or barbecue), in batches, until browned all over and cooked as desired.
3 Gently toss octopus and watercress in large bowl. Serve with lemon wedges, if desired.

serves 4
per serving 23.4g fat; 1985kJ (475 cal)

2 teaspoons coriander seeds, crushed
1.5kg cleaned baby octopus
⅓ cup (80ml) olive oil
2 cloves garlic, crushed
2 tablespoons lemon juice
2 tablespoons sweet chilli sauce
100g watercress, trimmed

salmon in sesame crust

PREPARATION TIME   **COOKING TIME**

2 cups (400g) medium-grain
   white rice
2 tablespoons sesame seeds
1 teaspoon coriander seeds
1 teaspoon black peppercorns
4 skinless salmon fillets (880g)
1 tablespoon vegetable oil
1 tablespoon sesame oil
1 clove garlic, crushed
1cm piece fresh ginger (5g),
   grated finely
1 small fresh red thai chilli,
   seeded, sliced thinly lengthways
500g baby bok choy,
   quartered lengthways
¼ cup (60ml) salt-reduced
   soy sauce
1 tablespoon mirin
2 tablespoons honey
2 tablespoons lime juice

1 Cook rice in large saucepan of boiling water, uncovered, until
   just tender; drain. Cover to keep warm.
2 Meanwhile, place seeds and peppercorns in strong plastic
   bag; crush with rolling pin or meat mallet. Coat one side of
   each fish fillet with seed mixture.
3 Heat vegetable oil in large frying pan; cook fish, seeded-side
   down, uncovered, for 1 minute. Turn; cook, uncovered, until
   fish is cooked as desired.
4 Meanwhile, heat sesame oil in wok; stir-fry garlic, ginger
   and chilli until fragrant. Add remaining ingredients; stir-fry
   until bok choy just wilts.
5 Serve fish with rice and bok choy.

serves 4
per serving 28.9g fat; 3546kJ (848 cal)

tomato, olive and anchovy pasta

PREPARATION TIME   **COOKING TIME**

500g garganelli pasta

½ cup (125ml) extra virgin olive oil

2 cloves garlic, crushed

1 teaspoon dried oregano leaves

6 anchovy fillets, drained,
   chopped finely

4 medium vine-ripened tomatoes
   (800g), chopped finely

2 tablespoons drained
   baby capers

½ cup (60g) seeded
   black olives, halved

1 Cook pasta in large saucepan of boiling water, uncovered, until just tender; drain, return to pan.

2 Meanwhile, heat oil in large frying pan; cook garlic, oregano and anchovy until fragrant. Add tomato, capers and olives; cook, stirring, until heated through.

3 Add sauce to pasta; toss thoroughly. Divide pasta among serving bowls.

serves 4

per serving 30.7g fat; 3029kJ (723 cal)

TIPS Recipe can be served warm or cold as a salad. Garganelli resembles a small, ridged, rolled tube. Penne pasta may be substituted.

prawns and fetta in garlic tomato sauce

PREPARATION TIME   **COOKING TIME**

1 Peel and devein prawns, leaving tails intact.
2 Heat oil in large frying pan; add onion and garlic, cook, stirring, until soft. Add wine; bring to a boil. Add undrained tomatoes, simmer, uncovered about 10 minutes or until thickened, stirring occasionally.
3 Stir in prawns, ¼ cup of the parsley and the oregano; simmer, uncovered, until prawns are just cooked through.
4 Transfer mixture to ovenproof dishes or one large ovenproof dish, sprinkle top with cheese. Grill until cheese is browned lightly.
5 Sprinkle with remaining parsley. Serve with crusty bread, if desired.

serves 4
per serving 25.3g fat; 2124kJ (507 cal)
TIP The tomato sauce can be made a day ahead; reheat, then add prawns just before serving.

1.5kg medium uncooked prawns
2 tablespoons olive oil
1 large brown onion (200g),
   chopped finely
4 cloves garlic, chopped finely
⅔ cup (160ml) dry white wine
2 x 425g cans crushed tomatoes
½ cup coarsely chopped
   fresh flat-leaf parsley
⅓ cup coarsely chopped
   fresh oregano
250g fetta cheese

swordfish with tomato and potato salad

PREPARATION TIME **COOKING TIME**

500g baby chat potatoes, halved

250g green beans, trimmed

4 swordfish fillets (800g)

2 tablespoons plain flour

250g cherry tomatoes, halved

¼ cup (40g) coarsely chopped
    seeded black olives

1 tablespoon coarsely chopped
    fresh dill

2 teaspoons finely grated
    lemon rind

1 tablespoon lemon juice

¼ cup (60ml) olive oil

1 Place potato in medium saucepan; pour over enough boiling water to cover. Boil, covered, for 10 minutes. Add beans to the same pan; cook, covered, until tender. Drain.

2 Meanwhile, toss fish in flour; shake away excess flour. Cook fish on a heated oiled grill pan (or grill or barbecue) until browned and cooked as desired.

3 In large bowl, combine tomato, olives, dill, rind, juice and oil; toss potato with tomato mixture.

4 Serve beans topped with fish and potato mixture.

serves 4

per serving 19.7g fat; 1964kJ (469 cal)

TIP Recipe is best made just before serving.

spicy squid salad

PREPARATION TIME ~~15 MINUTES (PLUS REFRIGERATION TIME)~~ **COOKING TIME** ~~5 MINUTES~~

Mizuna is a mild-tasting, crinkled salad leaf originating in Japan. It has a delicate mustard flavour. Mesclun also can be used in this recipe, if preferred.

6 squid hoods (900g)
2 tablespoons finely chopped
   fresh lemon grass
½ cup (125ml) sweet chilli sauce
1 clove garlic, crushed
2 tablespoons peanut oil
¼ cup (60ml) lemon juice
100g mizuna
1 cup (80g) bean sprouts
⅓ cup firmly packed fresh
   mint leaves
3 medium tomatoes (450g),
   seeded, chopped finely

1 Cut squid hoods down centre to open out, cut into three triangles; lightly score the inside of each squid triangle in a diagonal pattern. Combine in medium bowl with lemon grass, sauce, garlic, oil and juice, cover; refrigerate 3 hours or overnight.

2 Drain squid over small saucepan; reserve marinade. Cook squid, in batches, on heated oiled grill plate (or grill or barbecue) until browned all over and cooked through. Cover to keep warm.

3 Meanwhile, combine mizuna, sprouts, mint and tomato in large bowl. Bring reserved marinade to a boil; boil, uncovered, 1 minute.

4 Serve salad topped with squid; drizzle with hot marinade.

serves 6
per serving 8.6g fat; 869kJ (208 cal)

spiced fish with lemon yogurt sauce

PREPARATION TIME **COOKING TIME**

1 Cook rice in large saucepan of boiling water, uncovered, until tender; drain.
2 Meanwhile, heat large lightly oiled frying pan; cook lemon, uncovered, until lightly browned both sides. Remove from pan.
3 Combine spices and flour in small bowl; sprinkle over fish.
4 Heat oil in same pan; cook fish, uncovered, until browned both sides and cooked as desired.
5 Meanwhile, boil, steam or microwave carrots until just tender; drain.
6 Combine yogurt, juice and coriander in small bowl. Serve fish on rice with lemon, carrots and yogurt mixture.

serves 4
per serving 9.5g fat; 2594kJ (619 cal)
TIP We used perch in this recipe, but you can use any firm fish, such as ling or blue eye.

2 cups (400g) long-grain
  white rice
1 medium lemon, sliced thinly
1 teaspoon ground cumin
1 teaspoon ground cinnamon
2 teaspoons hot paprika
1 tablespoon plain flour
4 skinless white fish fillets (800g)
1 tablespoon olive oil
400g baby carrots
¾ cup (200g) low-fat yogurt
1 tablespoon lemon juice
2 tablespoons coarsely chopped
  fresh coriander

roasted pumpkin and spinach risotto

PREPARATION TIME 15 MINUTES **COOKING TIME** 50 MINUTES

500g pumpkin, chopped coarsely
2 tablespoons olive oil
1.25 litres (5 cups) water
1½ cups (375ml) vegetable stock
1 large brown onion (200g),
  chopped coarsely
2 cloves garlic, crushed
2 cups (400g) arborio rice
½ cup (125ml) dry white wine
250g spinach, chopped coarsely
½ cup (80g) toasted pine nuts
½ cup (40g) finely grated
  parmesan cheese
½ cup (125ml) cream

1 Preheat oven to hot.
2 Combine pumpkin and half of the oil in medium baking dish; roast, uncovered, in hot oven about 20 minutes or until tender.
3 Meanwhile, combine the water and stock in large saucepan; bring to a boil. Reduce heat; simmer, covered.
4 Heat remaining oil in large saucepan; cook onion and garlic, stirring, until onion softens. Add rice; stir to coat rice in oil mixture. Add wine; cook, stirring, until liquid is almost evaporated. Stir in ½ cup simmering stock mixture; cook, stirring, over low heat until liquid is absorbed. Continue adding stock mixture, in 1-cup batches, stirring until absorbed after each addition. Total cooking time should be about 35 minutes or until rice is just tender.
5 Add spinach, nuts, cheese and cream to risotto; cook, stirring, until spinach wilts. Add pumpkin; stir gently into risotto.

serves 4
per serving 41.4g fat; 3498kJ (837 cal)

spaghettini with rocket and sun-dried capsicum

PREPARATION TIME 10 MINUTES **COOKING TIME** 15 MINUTES

500g spaghettini pasta

270g jar sun-dried capsicums

¼ cup (60ml) olive oil

½ cup (80g) toasted pine nuts,
   chopped coarsely

2 small fresh red thai chillies,
   seeded, chopped finely

2 cloves garlic, crushed

100g rocket leaves,
   shredded finely

⅓ cup (25g) coarsely grated
   parmesan cheese

1 Cook pasta in large saucepan of boiling water, uncovered, until just tender; drain.

2 Meanwhile, drain capsicum over small bowl; reserve ¼ cup of the oil. Coarsely chop ½ cup of the capsicum; return remaining capsicum and oil to jar, keep for another use.

3 Heat reserved oil with olive oil in large saucepan; cook pine nuts, chilli and garlic, stirring, until fragrant. Add pasta, chopped capsicum and rocket; toss until rocket is just wilted.

4 Serve pasta sprinkled with cheese.

serves 4
per serving 49.3g fat; 4109kJ (983 cal)

baked three cheese pasta

PREPARATION TIME   **COOKING TIME**

1 Preheat oven to moderate.

2 Cook pasta in large saucepan of boiling water, uncovered, until just tender; drain.

3 Meanwhile, heat cream and stock in medium saucepan until hot. Remove from heat, add fontina, gorgonzola and half the parmesan; stir until melted. Add mustard and herbs. Combine cream mixture with drained pasta.

4 Pour pasta mixture into 2.5 litre (10-cup) ovenproof dish. Top with remaining parmesan. Bake in moderate oven about 20 minutes or until browned.

serves 4

per serving 54g fat; 3740kJ (893 cal)

TIP Recipe is best made close to serving.

375g macaroni pasta

300ml cream

⅓ cup (80ml) vegetable stock

1¼ cups (125g) grated
    fontina cheese

⅓ cup (75g) crumbled
    gorgonzola cheese

1¼ cups (100g) coarsely grated
    parmesan cheese

1 teaspoon dijon mustard

2 tablespoons finely chopped
    fresh flat-leaf parsley

1 tablespoon finely chopped
    fresh chives

potato and rosemary pizza

PREPARATION TIME 30 MINUTES (PLUS STANDING TIME)   **COOKING TIME** 15 MINUTES

2 teaspoons (7g) dry yeast

½ teaspoon caster sugar

¾ cup (180ml) warm water

2 cups (300g) plain flour

1 teaspoon salt

2 tablespoons extra virgin olive oil

2 tablespoons polenta

4 small potatoes (480g),
    sliced thinly

2 tablespoons fresh rosemary

2 cloves garlic, crushed

1 tablespoon extra virgin
    olive oil, extra

1 Combine yeast, sugar and the water in small bowl; cover, stand in a warm place about 10 minutes or until frothy.

2 Sift flour and salt into large bowl. Stir in yeast mixture and olive oil; mix to a soft dough. Bring dough together with hands; add a little extra water if necessary.

3 Knead dough on lightly floured surface about 10 minutes or until smooth and elastic. Place dough in lightly oiled large bowl; cover, stand in warm place about 1 hour or until doubled in size.

4 Preheat oven to very hot.

5 Punch dough down with your fist, then knead on lightly floured surface until smooth. Divide dough in half. Roll each half to a 20cm x 35cm rectangle, then place on oiled rectangular trays. Sprinkle with polenta; prick bases with a fork.

6 Layer potato, overlapping slightly, over top of pizza. Sprinkle with rosemary, drizzle with combined garlic and extra oil.

7 Bake on lowest shelf in very hot oven about 15 minutes or until base and potato are browned and crisp. Sprinkle with salt before serving.

serves 4

per serving 14.8g fat; 1926kJ (460 cal)

TIPS This recipe is best made close to serving.
The dough can be made in a breadmaker, following the manufacturer's instructions.

baked tortellini and vegetables

PREPARATION TIME ... **COOKING TIME** ...

500g cheese and spinach tortellini

1 tablespoon olive oil

200g mushrooms, sliced thinly

2 medium zucchini (240g),
chopped coarsely

1 medium red capsicum (200g),
chopped coarsely

700g bottled tomato pasta sauce

4 green onions, sliced thinly

¼ cup coarsely chopped fresh
flat-leaf parsley

2 cups (250g) coarsely grated
cheddar cheese

1 Preheat oven to moderately hot.

2 Cook pasta in large saucepan of boiling water, uncovered, until just tender; drain, reserve ½ cup of the cooking liquid.

3 Meanwhile, heat oil in large frying pan; cook mushroom, zucchini and capsicum, stirring, until vegetables are just tender. Stir in sauce and reserved cooking liquid; add pasta, onion and parsley, toss to combine.

4 Place tortellini mixture into deep oiled 3-litre (12-cup) ovenproof dish; sprinkle with cheese. Bake, uncovered, in moderately hot oven about 20 minutes or until lightly browned.

serves 4

per serving 35.7g fat; 3069kJ (734 cal)

TIPS Recipe can be assembled several hours before being reheated and browned in the oven.

Any filled pasta, such as agnolotti, ravioli or fagottini, can be used instead of tortellini.

potato and vegetable curry

PREPARATION TIME   **COOKING TIME**

1 Heat oil in large saucepan; cook onion, garlic, ginger and chilli, stirring, until onion softens. Add spices; cook, stirring, about 2 minutes or until fragrant. Add potato and pumpkin; stir to coat vegetables in spice mixture.

2 Stir in stock and coconut milk; bring to a boil. Reduce heat; simmer, covered, about 20 minutes or until potato is almost tender. Stir in beans; simmer, covered, about 5 minutes or until potato is just tender. Remove from heat; stir in spinach.

serves 4
per serving 24g fat; 1858kJ (444 cal)
TIP We used desiree potatoes, but whole new potatoes, also known as chats, are equally as good.

2 tablespoons vegetable oil
1 medium brown onion (150g), chopped finely
2 cloves garlic, crushed
5cm piece fresh ginger (25g), grated finely
2 small fresh red thai chillies, seeded, chopped finely
2 teaspoons ground cumin
2 teaspoons ground coriander
1 teaspoon garam masala
1 teaspoon ground turmeric
1kg potatoes, chopped coarsely
600g pumpkin, chopped coarsely
2 cups (500ml) vegetable stock
1 cup (250ml) coconut milk
200g green beans, halved
100g baby spinach leaves

gnocchi with burnt butter and tomato

PREPARATION TIME MINUTES (PLUS REFRIGERATION TIME) **COOKING TIME** MINUTES

3 large potatoes (900g),
   peeled, chopped coarsely

1 clove garlic, crushed

2 tablespoons milk

2 egg yolks

⅓ cup (25g) finely grated
   parmesan cheese

1 cup (150g) plain flour,
   approximately

100g butter, chopped coarsely

⅓ cup baby basil leaves

3 medium egg tomatoes (225g),
   chopped coarsely

1 Boil or steam potato until tender; drain. Cool potato slightly, mash with a masher, ricer or mouli until smooth; stir in garlic and milk. Stir in egg yolks, cheese and enough of the sifted flour to form a firm dough.

2 On a lightly floured surface, roll a quarter of the dough into 2cm thick log. Cut log into 1.5cm lengths and shape each into an oval. Press and roll dough with a floured fork to mark one side of gnocchi. Place on lightly floured tray in single layer. Repeat with remaining dough. Cover; refrigerate 1 hour.

3 Cook gnocchi, in batches, in large saucepan of boiling water about 3 minutes or until they float to the surface. Remove with a slotted spoon; drain well.

4 Meanwhile, melt butter in medium frying pan, add basil leaves; cook until crisp. Remove basil from pan with a slotted spoon; drain on absorbent paper. Add tomato; cook, stirring, until tomato softens.

5 Combine drained gnocchi and tomato mixture in large bowl, toss gently. Divide among serving dishes, sprinkle with basil. Serve with extra grated parmesan, if desired.

serves 4
per serving 26.2g fat; 2203kJ (526 cal)
TIP Uncooked gnocchi can be made six hours ahead.

sesame tofu on asian greens

PREPARATION TIME   **COOKING TIME**

600g firm tofu

⅓ cup (50g) sesame seeds

2 tablespoons cornflour

2 tablespoons sweet chilli sauce

⅓ cup (80ml) peanut oil

3 baby bok choy (450g),
   chopped coarsely

150g snow peas, halved

6 green onions, cut into lengths

1 large fresh red chilli, seeded,
   sliced thinly

SOY DRESSING

¼ cup (60ml) peanut oil

2 tablespoons soy sauce

¼ cup (60ml) rice vinegar

2 teaspoons brown sugar

1 clove garlic, crushed

1 tablespoon finely chopped
   fresh garlic chives

1 Cut tofu in half horizontally, then in half widthways.

2 Combine sesame seeds and cornflour in shallow bowl. Brush
   each piece of tofu with chilli sauce. Press tofu pieces into sesame
   mixture to coat.

3 Heat oil in large frying pan; cook tofu, in batches, until browned
   lightly all over. Drain on absorbent paper.

4 Steam or microwave bok choy, snow peas and onion until just
   tender. Arrange vegetables on serving plates, top with chilli and
   drizzle with half the soy dressing.

5 Serve tofu on vegetables, drizzled with the remaining dressing and
   topped with extra chives, if desired.

   SOY DRESSING Combine ingredients in screw-top jar; shake well.

serves 4

per serving 49.7g fat; 2494kJ (596 cal)

TIPS Recipe is best made just before serving.
The tofu can be coated an hour ahead.

chilli tofu and noodle salad

PREPARATION TIME 15 MINUTES (PLUS REFRIGERATION TIME)

1 Combine juice and sauces in screw-topped jar; shake well. Place half of the dressing in large bowl with tofu; stir to coat tofu all over in dressing. Cover; refrigerate 1 hour.

2 Meanwhile, using vegetable peeler or sharp knife, cut carrot, cucumber, onion and ginger into long, thin strips.

3 Place noodles in medium heatproof bowl; cover with boiling water. Stand until just tender; drain.

4 Combine noodles and vegetables with tofu. Add nuts, herbs, chilli and remaining dressing; toss gently to combine.

serves 4

per serving 14.8g fat; 1500kJ (358 cal)

TIP Kecap manis, found at Asian food stores and some supermarkets, is an Indonesian-style thick soy sauce that has sugar and spices added.

¼ cup (60ml) lime juice

2 tablespoons sweet chilli sauce

1 tablespoon fish sauce (optional)

2 teaspoons kecap manis

300g firm tofu, chopped coarsely

1 large carrot (180g)

1 lebanese cucumber (130g)

4 green onions

5cm piece fresh ginger (25g), grated finely

250g bean thread noodles

½ cup (75g) unsalted roasted cashews

2 tablespoons coarsely chopped fresh coriander

2 tablespoons coarsely chopped fresh mint

2 tablespoons coarsely chopped fresh thai basil

1 small fresh red thai chilli, seeded, sliced thinly

Side dishes are a quick and easy way to spice up an ordinary meal. Utilise the best and freshest ingredients for their textures, full flavours and gorgeous colours. Today's local fresh-food markets offer an astonishing assortment of fresh produce from which to choose, so there is no end of dishes you can make. Prepared at the same time as your main meal, these simple side dishes will transform your favourite recipe into an appetising main meal for the family.

rosemary potatoes

PREPARATION TIME 15 MINUTES **COOKING TIME** 1 HOUR 15 MINUTES

10 large potatoes (3kg)
2 tablespoons olive oil
1 tablespoon fresh rosemary leaves

1 Preheat oven to moderate.
2 Make 1cm cuts in each potato, slicing about three-quarters of the way through. Combine potatoes with oil in large baking dish, sprinkle with salt and pepper.
3 Bake in moderate oven about 1 hour. Increase oven temperature to hot, bake about 15 minutes or until potatoes are browned and tender. Sprinkle with rosemary.

serves 10
per serving 3.9g fat; 954kJ (228 cal)
TIPS We used desiree potatoes in this recipe.
Recipe is best made just before serving.

leeks, zucchini and asparagus with chive butter

PREPARATION TIME   **COOKING TIME**

1 Bring stock to a boil in large shallow frying pan; add leek and zucchini. Reduce heat and simmer gently, uncovered, 3 minutes.

2 Add asparagus, simmer, 3 minutes or until vegetables are just tender, turning occasionally; drain.

3 Melt butter in same frying pan, add garlic and chives. Return vegetables to pan and toss to coat them evenly in butter mixture.

serves 4
per serving 11.9g fat; 678kJ (162 cal)
TIP Recipe is best made close to serving.

1 litre (4 cups) vegetable stock
4 small leeks (800g),
   halved lengthways
8 small zucchini (720g),
   halved lengthways
200g asparagus, trimmed
50g butter
1 clove garlic, crushed
2 tablespoons chopped
   fresh chives

asparagus with anchovies and garlic

PREPARATION TIME
COOKING TIME

200g asparagus, trimmed
2 tablespoons olive oil
1 clove garlic, sliced thinly
3 anchovies, drained,
   chopped coarsely

1 Preheat oven to moderately hot.
2 Place asparagus in shallow baking
   dish; pour over combined oil, garlic
   and anchovies. Toss asparagus to
   coat in oil mixture.
3 Roast asparagus, uncovered,
   in moderately hot oven about
   5 minutes or until just tender.

serves 2
per serving 18.8g fat; 773kJ (185 cal)
TIP This recipe is best made close
to serving.

asparagus with butter and parmesan

PREPARATION TIME
COOKING TIME

200g asparagus, trimmed
20g butter, melted
2 tablespoons parmesan
   cheese flakes

1 Bring water to a boil in large frying
   pan; add asparagus, simmer,
   uncovered, about 2 minutes or
   until just tender; drain.
2 Serve drizzled with melted butter
   and sprinkled with cheese.

serves 2
per serving 10.4g fat; 479kJ (114 cal)
TIP This recipe is best made close
to serving.

asparagus with balsamic dressing

PREPARATION TIME
COOKING TIME

200g asparagus, trimmed
2 tablespoons olive oil
3 teaspoons balsamic vinegar
1 medium tomato (150g), peeled,
   seeded, chopped finely
1 tablespoon small basil leaves

1 Cook asparagus on heated, lightly
   oiled grill plate (or grill or barbecue)
   about 5 minutes or until tender.
2 Serve drizzled with combined oil,
   vinegar and tomato; sprinkle with
   basil leaves.

serves 2
per serving 18.3g fat; 748kJ (178 cal)
TIPS The dressing can be made
several days ahead.
The asparagus can be served hot
or at room temperature.

baby spinach and radicchio salad

PREPARATION TIME 10 MINUTES (PLUS STANDING TIME) **COOKING TIME** 5 MINUTES

¼ cup (40g) raisins
⅓ cup (80ml) olive oil
2 tablespoons red wine vinegar
1 medium radicchio lettuce (200g)
100g baby spinach leaves
¼ cup (40g) pine nuts, toasted

1 Combine raisins, oil and vinegar in small jar; shake well. Stand 1 hour.
2 Wash and dry lettuce and spinach leaves.
3 Just before serving, toss pine nuts and dressing through the combined salad leaves.

serves 10
per serving 10.4g fat; 538kJ (128 cal)
TIPS The dressing can be made several hours ahead.
The salad is best combined just before serving.

mixed garlic mushrooms

PREPARATION TIME ... MINUTES **COOKING TIME** ...

1 Preheat oven to moderately hot.
2 Place flat mushrooms in large baking dish, drizzle with half the oil. Roast, uncovered, 10 minutes.
3 Add remaining mushrooms, oil and garlic; roast in moderately hot oven 15 minutes or until mushrooms are tender and browned lightly. Stir in parsley.

250g flat mushrooms
2 tablespoons olive oil
250g swiss brown mushrooms
250g button mushrooms
1 clove garlic, sliced thinly
¼ cup loosely packed fresh
    flat-leaf parsley leaves

serves 4
per serving 9.6g fat; 525kJ (125 cal)
TIP Recipe is best cooked close to serving.

oven-baked vegetable crisps

PREPARATION TIME 15 MINUTES **COOKING TIME** 1 HOURS

cooking-oil spray
4 medium parsnips (1kg)
4 medium potatoes (800g)
1 medium kumara (400g)
2 teaspoons sea salt

1 Preheat oven to moderately slow. Spray three oven trays with cooking-oil spray.

2 Using mandolin, v-slicer or sharp knife, cut parsnip into 2mm slices. Place parsnip, in single layer, on oven trays; lightly coat with cooking-oil spray.

3 Bake, uncovered, in moderately slow oven about 40 minutes or until browned both sides and crisp. Turn onto wire rack to cool; repeat with potato and kumara.

4 Sprinkle crisps with salt.

serves 8
per serving 1.3g fat; 555kJ (133 cal)
TIPS The thinner the slices, the faster they'll become crisp, so some crisps may need to be removed from the oven before others. If you don't have a fan-forced oven, rotate trays frequently to ensure the vegetable slices brown evenly.

steamed spinach

PREPARATION TIME 5 MINUTES **COOKING TIME** 5 MINUTES

800g baby spinach leaves
¼ cup (60ml) olive oil
2 tablespoons lemon juice

1 Steam or microwave spinach until just wilted; drain well.
2 Transfer spinach to serving dish; pour over combined oil and juice. Serve immediately.

serves 8
per serving 7.1g fat; 321kJ (77 cal)
TIP Recipe best made just before serving.

beetroot with garlic sauce (skorthalia)

PREPARATION TIME   **COOKING TIME**

1 Boil or steam unpeeled beetroot until tender; drain. Peel while still warm. Cut beetroot into wedges; sprinkle with salt.

2 Serve beetroot with garlic sauce.

 GARLIC SAUCE Boil or steam potato until tender; drain. Mash potato until smooth; cool. Blend or process garlic, salt, water and juice until smooth. Add oil in a thin stream while motor is operating; blend until thick. Stir in potato. (Do not blend or process potato.)

serves 8

per serving 9.2g fat; 595kJ (142 cal)

TIP Garlic sauce can be made several hours ahead.

6 medium beetroot (1kg), trimmed

GARLIC SAUCE

1 medium potato (200g),
  sliced thickly

4 cloves garlic, chopped coarsely

½ teaspoon salt

2 tablespoons cold water

1½ tablespoons lemon juice

⅓ cup (80ml) olive oil

mixed pea salad with mint dressing

PREPARATION TIME **COOKING TIME**

1 cup (160g) shelled fresh peas

250g sugar snap peas, trimmed

250g snow peas, trimmed

50g snow pea sprouts

100g fetta cheese, crumbled

2 tablespoons toasted pine nuts

¼ cup firmly packed fresh
   mint leaves

MINT DRESSING

1 teaspoon finely grated
   lemon rind

2 tablespoons lemon juice

¼ cup (60ml) olive oil

2 tablespoons coarsely chopped
   fresh mint

1 teaspoon caster sugar

1 Bring large saucepan of water to a boil; add shelled peas. Boil, uncovered, 1 minute. Add sugar snap peas, boil further 1 minute. Add snow peas, boil further 20 seconds or until the snow peas change colour; drain.

2 Place all the peas into large bowl of iced water until cold; drain well.

3 Gently toss drained peas with snow pea sprouts in large serving bowl; top with cheese, pine nuts and mint leaves.

4 Drizzle mint dressing over salad just before serving.
   MINT DRESSING Combine ingredients in screw-top jar; shake well.

serves 6

per serving 16.6g fat; 878kJ (210 cal)

TIPS You will need about 400g fresh peas in the pod for this recipe.

The salad and dressing can be prepared two hours ahead; refrigerate separately.

chinese broccoli in oyster sauce

PREPARATION TIME   **COOKING TIME**

1kg chinese broccoli
2 litres (8 cups) chicken stock
100g garlic chives
¼ cup (60ml) oyster sauce

1 Wash broccoli to remove any grit from stems; cut into 8cm lengths.
2 Bring stock to a boil in large saucepan. Cook broccoli stems, 2 minutes. Add broccoli leaves and chives, cook about 1 minute or until just wilted.
3 Drain vegetables, reserving 2 tablespoons of the stock.
4 Serve vegetables drizzled with combined oyster sauce and reserved stock.

serves 6
per serving 1.9g fat; 280kJ (67 cal)
TIP This recipe is best prepared just before serving.

garlicky beans with pine nuts

PREPARATION TIME   **COOKING TIME**

1 Boil, steam or microwave beans until just tender; drain. Add beans to large bowl of iced water; drain well. Place in large bowl.
2 Heat oil and garlic in small frying pan over low heat until garlic just changes colour. Add nuts; stir until heated through.
3 Drizzle mixture over beans.

400g baby beans, trimmed
¼ cup (60ml) olive oil
1 clove garlic, sliced thinly
2 tablespoons pine nuts,
   toasted, chopped

serves 4
per serving 18.9g fat; 803kJ (191 cal)
TIPS The beans can be served hot or cold.
This recipe can be prepared several hours ahead.
Add pine nut mixture close to serving.

pasta salad with garlic vinaigrette

PREPARATION TIME   **COOKING TIME**

Purple basil, also known as opal basil, has an intense aroma and longer shelf-life than sweet basil.

375g penne pasta

200g sun-dried tomatoes in oil

½ cup (80g) pine nuts,
   toasted, chopped coarsely

400g bocconcini,
   chopped coarsely

1 small red onion (100g),
   sliced thinly

12 fresh purple basil leaves, torn

12 fresh basil leaves, torn

2 cloves garlic, crushed

1 tablespoon dijon mustard

¼ cup (60ml) lemon juice

1 Cook pasta in large saucepan of boiling water, uncovered, until just tender; drain. Rinse under cold water; drain.

2 Meanwhile, drain tomatoes; reserve oil. Slice tomatoes thickly.

3 Combine pasta and tomato in large bowl with nuts, cheese, onion and both basils.

4 Combine reserved sun-dried tomato oil and remaining ingredients in screw-topped jar; shake well. Drizzle dressing over salad; toss gently to combine.

serves 6

per serving 22.8g fat; 2249kJ (537 cal)

TIPS This recipe should be assembled just before serving.
Use your favourite short pasta instead of the penne, if you like.

tomato, olive and fetta salad

PREPARATION TIME 15 MINUTES

400g grape tomatoes

250g yellow teardrop tomatoes

1¼ cups (200g) black olives

1 small red onion (100g)

2 small zucchini (180g)

¼ cup (60ml) olive oil

2 tablespoons lemon juice

2 cloves garlic, crushed

1 teaspoon fresh oregano leaves

100g fetta cheese, crumbled

1 Place tomatoes and olives in large bowl.

2 Thinly slice onion; halve zucchini lengthways, then slice thinly on the diagonal. Add onion and zucchini to bowl with tomatoes.

3 Place oil, juice, garlic and oregano in screw-top jar; shake well.

4 Just before serving, pour dressing over tomato salad; add cheese, toss gently to combine.

serves 6

per serving 14.3g fat; 775kJ (185 cal)

TIP Salad and dressing can be made several hours ahead.

rocket salad

PREPARATION TIME

1 Combine rocket and onion in large serving bowl.
2 Combine remaining ingredients in screw top jar; shake well.
3 Just before serving, pour dressing over salad and toss lightly.

serves 6
per serving 6.3g fat; 288kJ (68 cal)
TIPS Rocket can be washed and dried a day ahead; store
in an airtight container or sealed plastic bag in the refrigerator.
Dressing can be made a day ahead; store in a jar in the refrigerator.

200g rocket leaves
1 small red onion (100g),
    sliced thinly
2 tablespoons olive oil
1 tablespoon red or
    white wine vinegar
½ teaspoon dijon mustard
½ teaspoon sugar

grilled capsicum, fennel and red onion salad

PREPARATION TIME   **COOKING TIME**

2 baby fennel (260g),
   trimmed, quartered
1 small yellow capsicum (150g),
   sliced thickly
1 small red capsicum (150g),
   sliced thickly
2 small red onions (200g),
   cut into wedges
2 tablespoons olive oil
1 clove garlic, crushed

BALSAMIC DRESSING
1 tablespoon lemon juice
2 tablespoons olive oil
1 tablespoon balsamic vinegar
1 clove garlic, crushed
1 tablespoon chopped
   fresh oregano

1 Combine vegetables with oil and garlic; stand 30 minutes.
2 Cook vegetables on heated oiled grill plate (or grill or barbecue) until browned and tender.
3 Serve vegetables, warm or cold, drizzled with balsamic dressing.
   BALSAMIC DRESSING Combine ingredients in screw-top jar; shake well.

serves 4
per serving 18.4g fat; 825kJ (197 cal)
TIP Recipe can be prepared several hours ahead.

DESSERTS

There's no denying dessert is an enjoyable way to end a meal, and this wonderful collection of desserts will delight and satisfy even the sweetest tooth. As the crowning touch to an elegant dinner, or a satisfying end to a family meal, dessert is everyone's favourite course. Hot or cold, stylish or simple, there is something to suit every occasion. From chilling sorbets to sumptuous chocolate, this is one grand finale where everyone's a winner.

baked coconut custards

PREPARATION TIME   **COOKING TIME**

Malibu is a liqueur made of white rum
blended with coconut and sugar.

1⅔ cups (400ml) coconut milk
½ cup (125ml) cream
6 egg yolks
¼ cup (55g) caster sugar
2 tablespoons Malibu
⅓ cup (15g) flaked coconut, toasted

1 Preheat oven to slow.
2 Place coconut milk and cream in small saucepan; bring almost
   to a boil. Remove from heat; stand, covered, 5 minutes.
3 Whisk yolks and sugar in medium bowl until combined; gradually
   whisk in warm coconut milk mixture and liqueur. Divide mixture
   among six ½-cup (125ml) heatproof dishes.
4 Place dishes in large baking dish; add enough boiling water to
   come halfway up sides of dishes. Bake, uncovered, in slow oven
   about 45 minutes or until custard is set. Remove dishes from water;
   cool. Cover; refrigerate until cold.
5 Serve custard sprinkled with flaked coconut.

serves 6
per custard 30.2g fat; 1485kJ (355 cal)
TIP Malibu is optional and can be replaced with milk, if desired.
SERVING SUGGESTION Almond biscotti and cups of hot espresso
are the perfect accompaniments for this rich and luscious dessert.

caramel self-saucing pudding

PREPARATION TIME   **COOKING TIME**

1 Preheat oven to moderate. Grease 2-litre (8-cup) shallow ovenproof dish.
2 Combine flour, sugar, butter, milk and dates in small bowl; mix well. Spread mixture into prepared dish.
3 Make caramel sauce.
4 Pour caramel sauce slowly over back of spoon over batter in dish. Bake in moderate oven about 40 minutes or until centre is firm.
5 Serve immediately with cream or ice-cream, if desired.
   CARAMEL SAUCE Combine ingredients in medium heatproof jug; stir until sugar is dissolved and butter melted.

serves 6
per serving 12.1g fat; 1716kJ (410 cal)
   Recipe must be made close to serving as sauce will be absorbed if left to stand.

1 cup (150g) self-raising flour
¾ cup (165g) firmly packed
   brown sugar
20g butter, melted
½ cup (125ml) milk
4 fresh dates (75g), seeded,
   chopped finely

¾ cup (165g) firmly packed
   brown sugar
2 cups (500ml) boiling water
60g butter, chopped

light steamed chocolate-chip pudding with butterscotch sauce

PREPARATION TIME ~~~ MINUTES **COOKING TIME** ~~~ HOURS ~~ MINUTES

1 cup (150g) self-raising flour
1 cup (70g) stale breadcrumbs
¼ cup (55g) brown sugar
2 x 410g jars fruit mince
125g butter, melted
⅓ cup (80ml) dark crème de cacao
3 eggs, beaten lightly
½ cup (60g) toasted chopped
    pecans
100g dark eating chocolate,
    chopped coarsely

BUTTERSCOTCH SAUCE
200g butter, chopped
1 cup (220g) firmly packed
    brown sugar
300ml cream

1 Lightly grease 6-cup (1.5 litre) pudding basin; line base with baking paper.
2 Sift flour into medium bowl. Add remaining ingredients; mix well. Spoon mixture into prepared pudding basin and smooth top.
3 Lightly grease sheet of foil large enough to cover top of basin and extend 5cm over side. Top foil with sheet of baking paper. Fold 2cm pleat through centre of paper and foil. Place sheets, foil side up, over pudding basin, tie securely under rim with a double length of string. Scrunch excess foil and paper tightly under string.
4 Place basin in large saucepan with enough boiling water to come halfway up side of basin. Cover saucepan and bring to a boil; boil about 3½ hours, adding more boiling water whenever necessary to maintain water level. To test if pudding is cooked, insert a skewer through foil in top of pudding; if skewer comes out clean, pudding is ready.
5 Carefully remove basin from saucepan and stand for 10 minutes before turning out.
6 Meanwhile, make butterscotch sauce.
7 Serve warm pudding with butterscotch sauce.
    BUTTERSCOTCH SAUCE Combine ingredients in medium pan. Stir over medium heat until butter is melted. Bring to a boil and simmer, uncovered, about 3 minutes or until thickened slightly.

serves 8
per serving 63.3g fat; 4398kJ (1051 cal)
TIP Recipe can be made two days ahead; keep refrigerated. Reheat single serves in the microwave, or return pudding to steamer and steam, as per the cooking method, for about 1 hour or until hot. Reheat sauce in the microwave or in a pan over a low heat.

greek honey puffs

PREPARATION TIME

COOKING TIME

2 teaspoons (7g) dry yeast

1 cup (250ml) warm milk

2 tablespoons caster sugar

1 egg, beaten lightly

60g butter, melted

2 cups (300g) plain flour

vegetable oil for deep-frying

⅔ cup (230g) honey, warmed

¼ teaspoon ground cinnamon

¼ cup coarsely chopped
   toasted walnuts

1 Combine yeast, milk, sugar, egg and butter in large bowl; mix well. Gradually stir in sifted flour; beat until smooth.

2 Cover bowl and leave to stand in warm place for about 1½ hours or until batter doubles in size and bubbles appear on the surface.

3 Beat batter with a wooden spoon until smooth.

4 Deep-fry rounded teaspoons of batter, in batches, in hot oil, dipping spoon in hot oil before spooning mixture out of bowl. Turn puffs to brown evenly during frying. Drain puffs on absorbent paper.

5 Divide puffs among serving plates, drizzle with honey, sprinkle with cinnamon and walnuts.

serves 8

per serving 9.5g fat; 1404kJ (335 cal)

TIP Recipe is best made just before serving.

poached nashi in fragrant syrup

PREPARATION TIME   **COOKING TIME**

1 Peel nashi, leaving stems intact.
2 Combine the water and sugar in large saucepan; stir over heat, without boiling, until sugar dissolves. Add nashi, ginger, lemon grass, star anise and rind; bring to a boil. Reduce heat; simmer, covered, about 20 minutes or until nashi are just tender, turning nashi occasionally. Remove from heat; cool nashi in syrup.
3 Remove nashi; bring syrup to a boil. Reduce heat; simmer, uncovered, about 10 minutes or until syrup reduces by a third. Remove from heat. Stir in juice; cool.
4 Divide nashi among serving bowls; drizzle with syrup.

4 medium nashi (800g)

2 cups (500ml) water

1 cup (220g) caster sugar

6cm piece fresh ginger (30g),
   sliced thinly

2 stems lemon grass,
   cut into 3cm lengths

2 star anise

2 thick strips lemon rind

1 tablespoon lemon juice

serves 4

per serving 0.2g fat; 1214kJ (290 cal)

The star anise adds a subtle aniseed flavour; omit it if you prefer.

sticky date cake with butterscotch sauce

PREPARATION TIME 30 MINUTES **COOKING TIME** 55 MINUTES (PLUS STANDING TIME)

3¾ cups (635g) dried pitted dates

3 cups (750ml) hot water

2 teaspoons bicarbonate of soda

185g butter, chopped

2¼ cups (500g) firmly packed
   brown sugar

6 eggs

3 cups (450g) self-raising flour

½ cup (60g) coarsely chopped
   walnuts

½ cup (60g) coarsely chopped
   pecans

BUTTERSCOTCH SAUCE

2 cups (440g) firmly packed
   brown sugar

500ml thickened cream

250g butter, chopped

1 Preheat oven to moderate. Grease 26cm x 36cm baking dish;
   double-line base and long sides with baking paper, bringing paper
   5cm above edges of dish.

2 Combine dates and the water in medium saucepan; bring to a boil.
   Remove from heat; stir in soda. Stand 5 minutes. Blend or process
   date mixture until smooth.

3 Beat butter and sugar in large bowl with electric mixer until light and
   fluffy. Add eggs, one at a time, beating until combined between each
   addition. Stir in date mixture and flour; spread mixture into prepared
   dish, sprinkle with nuts. Bake, uncovered, in moderate oven about
   50 minutes. Stand cake in dish 10 minutes; turn onto wire rack, turn
   cake top-side up.

4 Meanwhile, make butterscotch sauce.

5 Brush surface of hot cake with ⅓ cup of the hot butterscotch sauce.
   Serve with remaining sauce.
   BUTTERSCOTCH SAUCE Stir ingredients in medium saucepan over
   heat, without boiling, until sugar dissolves; bring to a boil. Reduce heat;
   simmer 3 minutes.

serves 20

per serving 33.1g fat; 2368kJ (566 cal)

TIPS Cake is suitable to freeze. To defrost, wrap in foil and
reheat in moderately slow oven for 20 minutes.
Sauce is suitable to microwave.

silky chocolate mousse

PREPARATION TIME **COOKING TIME**

300g dark eating chocolate,
  chopped coarsely
50g butter
3 eggs, separated
1 tablespoon irish cream liqueur
¼ cup (55g) caster sugar
300ml thickened cream, whipped

1 Combine chocolate and butter in small saucepan; stir over low heat until smooth. Remove from heat.

2 Stir in egg yolks, one at a time, then liqueur; transfer mixture to large bowl. Cool to room temperature.

3 Beat egg whites in small bowl with electric mixer until soft peaks form. Gradually add sugar, 1 tablespoon at a time, beating until sugar dissolves between additions.

4 Meanwhile, fold cream into chocolate mixture, then fold in egg white mixture, in two batches. Divide chocolate mousse among eight ½-cup (125ml) serving dishes. Cover; refrigerate 2 hours or until set.

serves 8
per serving 32g fat; 1801kJ (430 cal)
TIPS This recipe is best made a day ahead.
The chocolate and butter mixture is suitable to microwave.

ice-cream with espresso and irish cream

PREPARATION TIME

1 Place coffee and the water in coffee plunger; stand 2 minutes, plunge coffee. Cool 5 minutes.
2 Divide ice-cream among serving glasses; Pour liqueur then coffee over ice-cream. Serve with wafer sticks.

serves 4

per serving 22.7g fat; 1708kJ (408 cal)

TIPS Recipe is best made just before serving. We used Bailey's Irish Cream in this recipe, but you can use any irish cream liqueur.

2 tablespoons ground
  espresso coffee
⅔ cup (160ml) boiling water
500ml vanilla ice-cream
½ cup (125ml) irish cream liqueur
4 chocolate-coated rolled
  wafer sticks (15g)

hot chocolate soufflés

PREPARATION TIME 15 MINUTES **COOKING TIME** 15 MINUTES

2 tablespoons caster sugar
200g dark eating chocolate, chopped
50g butter, chopped
3 egg yolks
7 egg whites
¼ cup (55g) caster sugar, extra
sifted cocoa powder or icing sugar mixture, for dusting

1 Preheat oven to moderately hot.

2 Grease eight ½-cup (125ml) ovenproof dishes. Place sugar in one of the dishes, turn dish to coat base and side. Tip excess sugar into next dish; repeat with all dishes. Place dishes on oven tray.

3 Combine chocolate and butter in large heatproof bowl over pan of simmering water; stir until melted. Remove bowl from heat; stir in egg yolks.

4 Beat egg whites in large bowl with electric mixer until soft peaks form; gradually add extra sugar, beating until dissolved between additions.

5 Using large balloon whisk, gently fold one third of egg white mixture into chocolate mixture, then gently fold in remainder of egg white mixture.

6 Divide soufflé mixture among prepared dishes; smooth tops level with tops of dishes. Bake in moderately hot oven about 12 minutes or until soufflés are puffed.

7 Dust soufflés quickly with sifted cocoa powder or icing sugar; serve immediately with vanilla ice-cream, if desired.

serves 8
per serving 25.7g fat; 1862kJ (445 cal)
TIP Recipe must be made just before serving.

hazelnut and raisin bread and butter pudding

PREPARATION TIME   **COOKING TIME**

¾ cup (100g) hazelnuts
2 cups (500ml) cream
1½ cups (375ml) milk
350g loaf ciabatta
50g butter, melted
½ cup (85g) raisins
4 eggs
⅔ cup (150g) caster sugar
½ teaspoon vanilla essence

1 Preheat oven to moderate.
2 Place hazelnuts on oven tray; bake about 8 minutes or until skins begin to split. Place nuts in tea towel and rub to remove skins. Chop nuts coarsely.
3 Bring cream, milk and hazelnuts to the boil in medium saucepan; cover and remove from heat. Stand 20 minutes.
4 Remove crust from base of bread. Cut bread into 1.5cm-thick slices; brush one side of each slice with butter. Arrange bread, butter side up, slightly overlapping, in shallow, 2-litre (8-cup) ovenproof dish; sprinkle with raisins between layers.
5 Whisk eggs, sugar and essence in large bowl until combined. Gradually whisk cream mixture into egg mixture until combined. Strain mixture into jug; reserve hazelnuts. Pour hot milk mixture over bread; sprinkle with reserved nuts.
6 Place dish in large baking dish; add boiling water to come halfway up sides of dish. Bake, uncovered, in moderate oven about 50 minutes or until just set.

serves 8
per serving 42.2g fat; 2613kJ (624 cal)
Recipe can be made several hours ahead.

roasted stone fruit with caramel

PREPARATION TIME   **COOKING TIME**

1 Preheat oven to moderately hot.
2 Combine butter, sugar and vanilla bean in large shallow ovenproof dish; place in oven until butter is melted.
3 Meanwhile, halve peaches, nectarines and apricots; remove seeds, leave plums whole. Place fruit in dish, cut side up; bake, in moderately hot oven, about 1 hour, turning fruit frequently and basting occasionally with caramel mixture, or until fruit is browned and tender.
4 Serve fruit drizzled with remaining caramel mixture.

serves 4
per serving 12.5g fat; 1141kJ (273 cal)
TIP Recipe can be made several hours ahead.

60g butter
½ cup (110g) firmly packed
   brown sugar
1 vanilla bean, halved lengthways
2 medium peaches (300g)
2 medium nectarines (340g)
2 medium apricots (100g)
2 medium plums (220g)

roast nectarine tart

PREPARATION TIME ~~10 MINUTES (PLUS REFRIGERATION TIME)~~ **COOKING TIME** ~~35 MINUTES (PLUS COOLING TIME)~~

8 small nectarines (1.5kg),
  halved, stone removed
¼ cup (60ml) orange juice
½ cup (110g) firmly packed
  brown sugar

PASTRY

1⅔ cup (250g) plain flour
⅔ cup (110g) icing sugar mixture
125g cold butter, chopped
1 egg yolk
1½ tablespoons cold water,
  approximately

CREME PATISSIERE

300ml thickened cream
1 cup (250ml) milk
½ cup (110g) caster sugar
1 vanilla bean
3 egg yolks
2 tablespoons cornflour
90g butter, chopped

1 Grease 19cm x 27cm loose-based flan tin. Make pastry.
2 Make crème pâtissière while pastry case is cooling.
3 Increase oven temperature to hot.
4 Place nectarines, in single layer, in large shallow baking dish; sprinkle with juice and sugar. Roast, uncovered, in hot oven about 20 minutes or until nectarines are soft. Cool.
5 Meanwhile, spoon crème pâtissière into pastry case, cover; refrigerate about 30 minutes or until firm. Top with nectarines.
PASTRY Blend or process flour, sugar and butter until combined. Add egg yolk and enough of the water to make ingredients just come together. Knead dough on floured surface until smooth. Cover; refrigerate 30 minutes. Preheat oven to moderate. Roll dough between sheets of baking paper until large enough to line prepared tin. Ease dough into prepared tin, press into sides; trim edges. Cover; refrigerate 30 minutes. Cover pastry case with baking paper, fill with dried beans or rice; place on oven tray. Bake, uncovered, in moderate oven 10 minutes. Remove paper and beans; bake, uncovered, in moderate oven about 10 minutes or until pastry case is browned lightly. Cool.
CREME PATISSIERE Combine cream, milk and sugar in medium saucepan. Split vanilla bean in half lengthways, scrape seeds into saucepan, then add pod; bring to a boil. Remove from heat; discard pod. Beat egg yolks in small bowl with electric mixer until thick and creamy; beat in cornflour. Gradually beat in hot cream mixture. Strain mixture into same cleaned saucepan; stir over heat until mixture boils and thickens. Remove from heat; whisk in butter. Cover surface of crème pâtissière with plastic wrap; cool to room temperature.

serves 8
per serving 40g fat; 2993 kJ (715 cal)
TIP Uncooked rice or dried beans used to weigh down the pastry are not suitable for eating. Use them every time you bake-blind; store in an airtight storage jar.

chocolate brownie with warm chocolate sauce

PREPARATION TIME   **COOKING TIME**

Tía Maria and Kahlúa are two coffee-flavoured liqueurs; either of them can be used in this recipe.

150g butter, chopped
300g dark eating chocolate, chopped coarsely
1½ cups (330g) firmly packed brown sugar
4 eggs, beaten lightly
1 cup (150g) plain flour
½ cup (120g) sour cream
½ cup (75g) toasted hazelnuts, chopped coarsely

WARM CHOCOLATE SAUCE

150g dark eating chocolate, chopped coarsely
300ml thickened cream
⅓ cup (75g) firmly packed brown sugar
2 teaspoons coffee-flavoured liqueur

1 Preheat oven to moderate. Grease 20cm x 30cm lamington pan; line base and sides with baking paper.

2 Stir butter and chocolate in small saucepan over low heat until mixture is smooth. Transfer to medium bowl.

3 Stir in sugar and egg, then flour, sour cream and nuts; spread mixture into prepared pan. Bake, uncovered, in moderate oven about 30 minutes. Cool in pan.

4 Meanwhile, make warm chocolate sauce.

5 Cut brownie into 16 pieces; serve drizzled with warm chocolate sauce.
WARM CHOCOLATE SAUCE Stir chocolate, cream and sugar in small saucepan over low heat until mixture is smooth. Remove from heat; stir in liqueur.

serves 8
per serving 59.7g fat; 4032kJ (963 cal)

berry custard pastries

PREPARATION TIME 40 MINUTES (PLUS REFRIGERATION TIME) **COOKING TIME** 12 MINUTES

2 sheets ready-rolled
    butter puff pastry
2 tablespoons icing sugar mixture
700g mixed fresh berries

CUSTARD CREAM
300ml thickened cream
300g thick vanilla custard
¼ cup (40g) icing sugar mixture

1 Preheat oven to hot. Grease and line three oven trays with baking paper.
2 Cut one pastry sheet in half. Sprinkle one half with 2 teaspoons of the sugar; place remaining half of the pastry on top. Roll pastry up tightly from short side; cut log into eight rounds. Repeat with remaining pastry sheet and another 2 teaspoons of the sugar.
3 Place rounds, cut-side up, on board dusted lightly with icing sugar; shape each round into an oval about 8cm x 10cm.
4 Place ovals on prepared trays. Bake, uncovered, in hot oven about 12 minutes or until pastries are browned lightly and crisp, turning halfway through baking.
5 Meanwhile, make custard cream.
6 Place a drop of the custard cream on each serving plate (to stop pastry sliding); top each with a pastry. Divide half of the berries over pastries, then top with custard cream, remaining berries and remaining pastries. Dust with sifted remaining sugar.

CUSTARD CREAM Beat cream, custard and sugar in small bowl with electric mixer until soft peaks form. Cover; refrigerate 30 minutes or until firm.

serves 8
per pastry 24.5g fat; 1538kJ (367 cal)
TIPS Recipe can be prepared a day ahead; assemble just before serving. Keep pastries in an airtight container; keep custard cream, covered, in refrigerator.
We used a mixture of fresh berries that included mulberries, strawberries, youngberries and blueberries.

italian ricotta cheesecake

PREPARATION TIME   **COOKING TIME**

1kg ricotta cheese

5 eggs, beaten lightly

1 tablespoon finely grated
    lemon rind

¼ cup (60ml) lemon juice

1 teaspoon vanilla essence

1 cup (220g) caster sugar

¼ cup (40g) sultanas

½ cup (125g) finely chopped
    mixed glacé fruit

PASTRY

90g butter, softened

1 egg

¼ cup (55g) caster sugar

1¼ cups (185g) plain flour

¼ cup (35g) self-raising flour

1 Grease 25cm springform tin. Make pastry.

2 Reduce oven temperature to moderately slow.

3 Blend or process cheese, egg, rind, juice, essence and sugar
    until smooth. Stir in sultanas and glacé fruit; pour cheesecake
    filling over pastry base.

4 Bake cheesecake, uncovered, in moderately slow oven about
    50 minutes or until filling sets; cool at room temperature, then
    refrigerate until cold.
    PASTRY Beat butter in small bowl with electric mixer until smooth;
    add egg and sugar, beating until just combined. Stir in half of the
    combined sifted flours; work remaining flour in by hand. Knead
    pastry gently on floured surface until smooth. Cover with plastic
    wrap; refrigerate 30 minutes. Preheat oven to moderately hot. Roll
    pastry between sheets of baking paper until large enough to cover
    base of prepared tin. Lift pastry into tin; press into base. Lightly prick
    pastry with fork, cover; refrigerate 30 minutes. Bake, uncovered, in
    moderately hot oven 20 minutes.

serves 16

per serving 13.7g fat; 1262kJ (301 cal)

TIP Recipe is best made a day ahead; store, covered,
in refrigerator overnight.

chocolate ganache meringue

PREPARATION TIME **COOKING TIME**

3 egg whites
¾ cup (165g) caster sugar
1 tablespoon cocoa powder
1½ cups (375ml) thickened cream
1 tablespoon icing sugar mixture
1 teaspoon vanilla essence
cocoa powder, extra, for dusting

GANACHE
100g dark eating chocolate,
   chopped
½ cup (125ml) thickened cream

1 Preheat oven to very slow. Line three oven trays with a piece of baking paper. Draw 8cm x 25cm rectangle on each piece of paper; turn it over.
2 Beat egg whites in small bowl with electric mixer until soft peaks form. Gradually add caster sugar, beating until dissolved between additions. Fold in sifted cocoa powder.
3 Spread mixture evenly over rectangles. Bake in very slow oven about 45 minutes or until firm. Cool in oven with the door ajar.
4 Make ganache.
5 Meanwhile, beat cream, icing sugar and essence in small bowl with electric mixer until soft peaks form.
6 Place one meringue layer on serving plate; spread with half the ganache; top with half of the whipped cream. Place another meringue layer on top of the cream; repeat layers with remaining ganache and cream. Top with remaining meringue layer, dust with extra sifted cocoa powder.
GANACHE Combine chocolate and cream in small saucepan; stir over low heat until smooth. Refrigerate until almost firm.

serves 8
per serving 26.9g fat; 1556kJ (372 cal)
TIP Meringue layers can be made four days ahead. Store in an airtight container in a cool, dry place. Assemble the meringue up to six hours before serving.

white chocolate and strawberry cheesecake

PREPARATION TIME   **COOKING TIME**

Butternut Snap biscuits, made from sugar, flour, rolled oats, butter, coconut and golden syrup, are similar to Anzac biscuits, and can be found at your local supermarket.

185g Butternut Snap biscuits
80g butter, melted
3 teaspoons gelatine
2 tablespoons water
2 x 250g packets cream cheese, softened
395g can sweetened condensed milk
300ml thickened cream
150g white eating chocolate, melted
500g large strawberries, halved
¼ cup (80g) strawberry jam, warmed, strained
1 tablespoon lemon juice

1 Grease 23cm springform tin.
2 Blend or process biscuits until mixture resembles fine breadcrumbs. Add butter; process until combined. Using hand, press biscuit mixture evenly over base of prepared tin, cover; refrigerate about 30 minutes or until firm.
3 Sprinkle gelatine over the water in small heatproof jug; stand jug in small saucepan of simmering water. Stir until gelatine dissolves. Cool 5 minutes.
4 Meanwhile, beat cheese and condensed milk in medium bowl with electric mixer until smooth. Beat cream in small bowl with electric mixer until soft peaks form.
5 Stir warm gelatine mixture into cheese mixture; fold in cream and chocolate. Pour cheesecake mixture into prepared tin, spreading evenly over biscuit base. Cover; refrigerate overnight.
6 Arrange strawberries on top of cheesecake; brush strawberries with combined jam and juice.

serves 10
per serving 47.3g fat; 2761kJ (660 cal)

hazelnut praline tiramisu

PREPARATION TIME 10 MINUTES (PLUS COOLING TIME)
COOKING TIME 10 MINUTES (PLUS REFRIGERATION AND STANDING TIME)

¼ cup (30g) ground coffee
2 cups (500ml) boiling water
1 cup (250ml) marsala
4 egg yolks
¼ cup (55g) caster sugar
1kg (4 cups) mascarpone
¼ cup (60ml) marsala, extra
½ cup (110g) caster sugar, extra
500g sponge finger biscuits
100g coarsely grated dark
    eating chocolate

HAZELNUT PRALINE
¼ cup (35g) hazelnuts
⅓ cup (75g) caster sugar
2 tablespoons water

1 Using the coffee and boiling water, prepare coffee in a plunger. Stand for 2 minutes, plunge coffee (or combine the coffee and water in a heatproof jug, stand for 2 minutes then strain through a fine sieve); pour into large jug, stir in liqueur.

2 Beat egg yolks and sugar in small bowl with electric mixer until fluffy.

3 Beat mascarpone, extra liqueur and extra sugar in large bowl until slightly thickened. Gently fold in egg yolk mixture.

4 Pour half the coffee mixture into shallow bowl. Dip half the biscuits, a couple at a time, into coffee mixture until beginning to soften. Line base of 3-litre (12-cup) rectangular serving dish with biscuits; brush with any unused coffee mixture. Spread biscuits with half the mascarpone mixture and sprinkle with half the grated chocolate. Repeat with remaining biscuits, coffee mixture and mascarpone.

5 Cover, refrigerate overnight.

6 Just before serving, sprinkle with remaining chocolate and chopped hazelnut praline.

HAZELNUT PRALINE Preheat oven to moderate. Place hazelnuts in shallow baking dish; bake about 8 minutes or until skins split. Rub nuts in tea towel to remove most of the skin, cool. Lightly grease an oven tray. Combine sugar and water in small saucepan; stir over low heat until sugar is dissolved. Brush sides of pan with pastry brush dipped in water to remove sugar crystals. Bring to a boil. Boil, uncovered, without stirring, about 5 minutes or until mixture turns a toffee colour. Remove from heat, stir in nuts then quickly pour onto prepared tray. Stand until set.

serves 15
per serving 44.4g fat; 2724kJ (651 cal)
TIPS Tiramisu is best prepared a day ahead. Hazelnut praline can be made several days ahead; store in an airtight container. Use a blender or food processor to roughly chop the praline.

roasted whole quinces

PREPARATION TIME ~~15 MINUTES~~   **COOKING TIME** ~~4 HOURS~~

1.5 litres (6 cups) water

1.5kg (7 cups) sugar

2.4kg whole quinces

1 strip orange rind

1 cinnamon stick

2 cardamom pods

¾ cup (180ml) lemon juice, approximately

1 Preheat oven to moderate.

2 Combine the water and sugar in medium saucepan. Stir over medium heat, without boiling, until sugar is dissolved.

3 Wash quince well. Put unpeeled quince, rind and spices into large ovenproof dish; pour syrup over. Cover dish, bake in moderate oven about 4 hours, turning occasionally, or until quinces are tender and deep pink. Remove quince, add enough juice to the syrup to adjust sweetness.

4 When cool enough to handle, peel skin from quince.

5 Serve warm quince with syrup and cream, if desired.

serves 6

per serving 0.86g fat; 4838kJ (1156 cal)

TIP Recipe can be made two days ahead. Gently rewarm quince and syrup before serving.

raspberry sorbet

PREPARATION TIME   **COOKING TIME**

1 Stir the water and sugar in small saucepan over heat, without boiling, until sugar dissolves; bring to a boil. Reduce heat, simmer, uncovered, without stirring, 5 minutes.
2 Blend or process raspberries, juice and hot sugar mixture until smooth.
3 Push mixture through fine sieve into 20cm x 30cm lamington pan; discard seeds. Cover with foil; freeze until firm.
4 Chop frozen berry mixture coarsely. Blend or process with egg whites until smooth and paler in colour. Return mixture to pan, cover; freeze until firm.

1 cup (250ml) water
1 cup (220g) caster sugar
600g frozen raspberries
1 tablespoon lemon juice
2 egg whites

serves 6
per serving 0.41g fat; 764kJ (182 cal)
TIPS If using an ice-cream churner, combine fruit puree with egg whites; churn, following manufacturer's instructions.
Recipe can be made a week ahead.
Raspberries may be replaced with any other berry.

chocolate, nut and coffee ice-cream cake

PREPARATION TIME 35 MINUTES (PLUS COOLING AND FREEZING TIME)

Vienna almonds are toffee-coated almonds available from selected supermarkets, nut stands and gourmet food and specialty confectionery stores. Crème de cacao is a chocolate-flavoured liqueur and can be found in most liquor stores.

2 litres vanilla ice-cream
1 tablespoon instant coffee powder
1 tablespoon hot water
½ cup (70g) vienna almonds, chopped coarsely
100g dark eating chocolate, melted
1 tablespoon crème de cacao
100g white eating chocolate, melted
½ cup (75g) roasted shelled pistachios, chopped coarsely

1 Grease 21cm springform tin; line base and side with baking paper.
2 Divide ice-cream into three portions; return two portions to freezer. Soften remaining ice-cream in medium bowl.
3 Dissolve coffee in the water in small jug, cool; stir into softened ice-cream with two-thirds of the almonds. Spoon into prepared tin, cover; freeze about 2 hours or until firm.
4 Meanwhile, soften second portion of the ice-cream in medium bowl; stir in dark chocolate. Microwave, uncovered, on MEDIUM-HIGH (80%) about 2 minutes or until chocolate melts; whisk until smooth. Stir in liqueur, cover; freeze about 1 hour or until almost firm. Spoon dark chocolate ice-cream over coffee layer, cover; freeze about 2 hours or until firm.
5 Soften remaining ice-cream in medium bowl; fold in white chocolate. Microwave, uncovered, on MEDIUM-HIGH (80%) about 2 minutes or until chocolate melts; whisk until smooth. Stir in two-thirds of the pistachios, cover; freeze about 1 hour or until almost firm, stirring ice-cream occasionally to suspend pistachios evenly. Spoon white chocolate ice-cream over dark chocolate layer, cover; freeze about 2 hours or until firm.
6 Remove ice-cream cake from tin just before serving; sprinkle with remaining almonds and pistachios.

serves 10
per serving 23.6g fat; 1591kJ (380 cal)
TIPS Use a good-quality ice-cream; various ice-creams differ from manufacturer to manufacturer, depending on the quantities of air and fat incorporated into the mixture.
It is important each layer sets firm before adding the next.
To remove ice-cream cake easily, rub sides of tin with a hot cloth.

crème catalana

PREPARATION TIME   **COOKING TIME**

8 egg yolks
1 cup (220g) caster sugar
1.125 litres (4½ cups) milk
2 teaspoons finely grated
   lemon rind
1 cinnamon stick
½ cup (75g) cornflour
⅓ cup (75g) caster sugar, extra

1 Beat yolks and sugar in large bowl with balloon whisk until creamy.
2 Combine 1 litre (4 cups) of the milk, rind and cinnamon in large saucepan; stir over medium heat until mixture just comes to a boil. Remove immediately from heat.
3 Strain milk into a large heatproof jug; pour milk into egg mixture, whisking constantly. Stir remaining milk and cornflour in small jug until smooth; add to egg mixture.
4 Return mixture to pan; stir constantly over heat until mixture boils and thickens.
5 Pour mixture into 26cm heatproof pie dish; cover, refrigerate 4 hours or overnight.
6 Just before serving, sprinkle with extra sugar. Grill until sugar is caramelised.

serves 8
per serving 9.3g fat; 1325kJ (316 cal)
TIPS Custard mixture can be made a day ahead.
Caramelise the sugar just before serving

lime delicious

PREPARATION TIME   **COOKING TIME**

1 Preheat oven to moderate. Grease deep 1.25-litre (5-cup) ovenproof dish.
2 Beat butter, rind, sugar and egg yolks in small bowl with electric mixer until mixture is creamy. Beat in sifted flour and juice, then gradually beat in milk.
3 In clean small mixing bowl, beat 4 egg whites until firm peaks form; fold through lime mixture.
4 Pour mixture into prepared dish. Place dish in larger baking dish containing cold water to come halfway up its side. Bake about 40 minutes or until browned and just firm.
5 Dust with sifted icing sugar and serve immediately with cream or ice-cream, if desired.

serves 6
per serving 8.4g fat; 826kJ (197 cal)
TIP Recipe must be made close to serving.

30g butter, softened
1 teaspoon grated lime rind
½ cup (110g) caster sugar
3 eggs, separated
¼ cup (35g) plain flour
½ cup (125ml) lime juice
1 cup (250ml) milk
1 egg white, extra
icing sugar, for dusting

mango passionfruit pavlova roll

PREPARATION TIME 15 MINUTES **COOKING TIME** 20 MINUTES (PLUS COOLING TIME)

4 egg whites

¾ cup (165g) caster sugar

1 teaspoon vanilla essence

1 teaspoon white vinegar

1 teaspoon cornflour

½ cup (25g) flaked coconut

300ml thickened cream

2 tablespoons passionfruit pulp

2 medium mangoes (860g),
   sliced thinly

1 Preheat oven to moderately slow. Grease 25cm x 30cm swiss roll pan, then place a piece of baking paper so that it covers the base and extends over the two opposite sides of the pan.

2 Beat egg whites in small bowl with electric mixer until soft peaks form; gradually add sugar, beating until dissolved between additions. Fold in essence, vinegar and cornflour.

3 Spread mixture into prepared pan; sprinkle with coconut. Bake on lower shelf in moderately slow oven about 20 minutes or until meringue is browned lightly.

4 Meanwhile, cover wire rack with sheet of baking paper. Invert meringue onto paper; remove lining paper, cool, coconut-side down.

5 Whip cream until soft peaks form; spread over cooled meringue. Top with passionfruit and mango.

6 Roll meringue firmly from long side, using baking paper to guide meringue as it rolls.

serves 8
per serving 15.9g fat; 1169kJ (279 cal)
TIPS You will need about two large passionfruit for this recipe.
Recipe can be made six hours ahead; cover and refrigerate.

rich chocolate tart

PREPARATION TIME   **COOKING TIME**

4 egg yolks

2 eggs

¼ cup (55g) caster sugar

⅓ cup (80ml) thickened cream

300g dark eating chocolate,
  melted

1 teaspoon vanilla essence

PASTRY

1¼ cups (185g) plain flour

¼ cup (25g) cocoa powder

⅓ cup (55g) icing sugar mixture

150g cold butter, chopped

2 egg yolks

1 teaspoon iced water

1 Make pastry.

2 Reduce oven temperature to moderately slow.

3 Beat egg yolks, eggs and caster sugar in small bowl with electric mixer
   until thick and creamy. Fold in cream, chocolate and essence.

4 Pour chocolate mixture into pastry case. Bake, uncovered, in moderately
   slow oven about 30 minutes or until filling is set. Cool 10 minutes. Serve
   tart dusted with a little extra sifted cocoa powder, if desired.

   PASTRY Blend or process flour, sifted cocoa powder, sugar and butter
   until combined. Add egg yolks and the water; process until ingredients
   just come together. Knead dough on floured surface until smooth. Cover
   with plastic wrap; refrigerate 30 minutes. Roll dough between sheets
   of baking paper until large enough to line base and side of greased
   24cm-round loose-based flan tin. Ease dough into tin, press into side;
   trim edge. Cover; refrigerate 30 minutes. Preheat oven to moderate. Cover
   pastry case with baking paper, fill with dried beans or rice; place on oven
   tray. Bake, uncovered, in moderate oven 15 minutes. Remove paper and
   beans; bake, uncovered, about 10 minutes or until browned lightly. Cool.

   serves 10
   per serving 28.3g fat; 1888kJ (451 cal)
   TIP Recipe can be made a day ahead.

frozen nectarine and turkish delight parfait

PREPARATION TIME

1 Line 14cm x 21cm loaf pan with a strip of foil or baking paper to cover the base and extend over the two long sides.
2 Beat ricotta and sugar in small bowl with electric mixer until smooth. Transfer ricotta mixture to large bowl.
3 Beat cream in small bowl with electric mixer until soft peaks form. Stir chocolate, turkish delight and nectarines into ricotta mixture; fold in cream.
4 Spoon mixture into prepared pan, smooth top; cover, freeze overnight or until firm.
5 Turn parfait out onto a board; slice. Stand at least 15 minutes or until softened slightly before serving. Decorate with extra chopped turkish delight, if desired.

2 cups (400g) ricotta cheese
¾ cup (165g) caster sugar
300ml thickened cream
100g white chocolate Toblerone,
  chopped finely
100g turkish delight,
  chopped finely
1 cup (150g) chopped nectarines

serves 6
per serving 31.5g fat; 2185kJ (522 cal)
TIP Recipe can be made two weeks ahead.

tangy lemon tart

PREPARATION TIME
COOKING TIME

1 cup (150g) plain flour
¼ cup (40g) icing sugar mixture
90g cold butter, chopped
1 egg, separated

FILLING
4 eggs
1 tablespoon finely grated
    lemon rind
¾ cup (180ml) lemon juice
¾ cup (165g) caster sugar
½ cup (125ml) thickened cream

1 Blend or process flour, icing sugar and butter until combined. Add egg yolk (reserve egg white for filling) and process until ingredients just start to come together. Knead dough lightly on floured surface until smooth; cover in plastic wrap, refrigerate 30 minutes.

2 Grease 24cm loose-based flan tin. Roll pastry between two sheets of baking paper until large enough to line prepared tin. Ease pastry into tin and press into side, trim edge. Place tin on oven tray and freeze for 15 minutes.

3 Meanwhile, preheat oven to moderate.

4 Cover pastry with baking paper and fill with dried beans or rice. Bake in moderate oven 15 minutes. Remove paper and beans, bake about 5 minutes or until browned lightly. Carefully shield sides of pastry with foil if over-browning.

5 Reduce oven temperature to slow.

6 Make filling.

7 Pour strained filling into pastry case, bake in slow oven about 25 minutes or until just set; cool. Refrigerate until cold.

8 Dust with sifted icing sugar and serve with cream, if desired.
FILLING Whisk eggs, egg white, rind, juice, sugar and cream in medium bowl.

serves 8
per serving 18.4g fat; 1465kJ (350 cal)
TIP Recipe can be prepared a day ahead.

layered mango sorbet and ice-cream cake

PREPARATION TIME

COOKING TIME

½ cup (110g) caster sugar
½ cup (125ml) water
2 tablespoons lime juice
2 medium mangoes (860g)
1 egg white, beaten lightly
1 litre vanilla ice-cream

1 Combine sugar and the water in small saucepan; stir over medium heat, without boiling, until sugar is dissolved. Add juice, bring to a boil; simmer, uncovered, 5 minutes. Cover, refrigerate until cold.

2 Process peeled and chopped mangoes until smooth. Add lime syrup and egg white; churn mixture in an ice-cream machine until firm. (Or, process until combined. Pour into a freezer-proof container; freeze until just set. Chop mixture, process again until creamy.)

3 Line base of deep 22cm cake pan with baking paper. Spread half the mango sorbet mixture into pan and smooth top; freeze several hours or until mixture is firm. Keep remaining sorbet in container in freezer.

4 Meanwhile, place vanilla ice-cream in refrigerator to soften. Spoon half the ice-cream over sorbet in pan; smooth the top. Freeze until firm.

5 Repeat with final two layers, processing sorbet again until smooth before using. Freeze until firm between layers.

6 To serve, rub outside of pan with a warm damp cloth. Invert pan onto serving plate. Top with candied lime slices, if desired.

serves 8
per serving 6.8g fat; 881kJ (210 cal)
TIP Recipe can be prepared up to a week ahead.

white chocolate frozen Christmas pudding

PREPARATION TIME

1 Line 17.5cm 1.75-litre (7-cup) pudding basin with plastic wrap, extending plastic 5cm over edge of basin.
2 Combine fruit and brandy in large bowl; stand 30 minutes.
3 Stir ice-cream and nuts into fruit mixture until combined. Pack ice-cream mixture into prepared basin, cover with foil; freeze overnight.
4 Turn pudding onto tray; remove plastic wrap, return pudding to freezer.
5 Cut a piece of paper into 35cm circle to use as a guide. Cover paper with a large sheet of plastic wrap. Spread chocolate over plastic wrap. Quickly drape plastic, chocolate-side down, over pudding. Smooth pudding with hands before gently peeling away plastic wrap. Trim base; centre pudding on serving plate. Return to freezer until ready to serve.

serves 12
per serving 27.3g fat; 1963kJ (469 cal)
TIPS Decorate pudding with frozen cherries and dust with icing sugar just before serving, if desired.
Recipe can be made one week ahead. Add chocolate coating up to three hours before serving.

Craisins are dried cranberries; they are sold in most supermarkets.

½ cup (75g) craisins
½ cup (115g) finely chopped glacé pineapple
¼ cup (60ml) brandy
2 litres vanilla ice-cream, softened
2 cups (280g) vienna almonds, chopped coarsely
360g white eating chocolate, melted

Many of us remember the wonderful aromas wafting from the kitchens of our grandmothers as they removed golden biscuits and warm, spicy cakes from the oven. This range of cakes, slices and biscuits will have your family and friends expressing the same enjoyment as they devour every crumb. These homemade delights are simple to make, and are just as good for entertaining as they are for morning tea or after-school treats.

macadamia and ginger fingers

PREPARATION TIME   **COOKING TIME**

125g butter, chopped
¼ cup (55g) caster sugar
1 cup (150g) self-raising flour
1 teaspoon ground ginger

MACADAMIA TOPPING

90g butter, chopped
2 tablespoons golden syrup
¾ cup (120g) icing sugar mixture
1 cup (150g) macadamias,
    toasted, chopped coarsely
¼ cup (50g) finely chopped
    glacé ginger

1 Preheat oven to moderate. Grease 20cm x 30cm lamington pan; line base and long sides of pan with baking paper, extending paper 2cm above edges of pan.
2 Beat butter and sugar in small bowl with electric mixer until light and fluffy. Add flour and ginger; beat on low speed until just combined.
3 Spread mixture evenly into prepared pan; bake in moderate oven about 15 minutes or until browned lightly. Cool to room temperature in pan.
4 Spread hot macadamia topping evenly over cooled base; bake in moderate oven about 10 minutes. Cool in pan before cutting into pieces.
   MACADAMIA TOPPING Combine butter, syrup and sugar in small saucepan; stir over heat until mixture is smooth. Stir in nuts and ginger.

makes 16
per finger 18.3g fat; 1086kJ (260 cal)
TIP Make sure the base has completely cooled to room temperature before spreading on the hot macadamia topping.

date and lemon slice

PREPARATION TIME   **COOKING TIME**

1 Make filling.
2 Preheat oven to moderate. Grease 20cm x 30cm lamington pan; line base and long sides of pan with baking paper, extending paper 2cm above edges of pan.
3 Sift flour into large bowl, rub in butter with fingertips. Stir in combined essence, rind and egg, then sugar, desiccated coconut and walnuts; mix well.
4 Press half of the flour mixture firmly over base of prepared pan. Spread filling over base. Add shredded coconut to remaining flour mixture then sprinkle over filling.
5 Bake in moderate oven about 35 minutes or until browned. Cool in pan before cutting into pieces.

DATE FILLING Combine dates, sugar and water in medium saucepan. Bring to a boil then simmer, stirring, about 3 minutes or until dates are pulpy. Stir in lemon juice; cool.

makes 16
per slice 13.3g fat; 1184kJ (383 cal)
Recipe can be made a day ahead; store in an airtight container.

1⅔ cups (250g) plain flour
150g butter, chopped
1 teaspoon vanilla essence
1 teaspoon finely grated lemon rind
1 egg, beaten lightly
¾ cup (165g) caster sugar
¾ cup (60g) desiccated coconut
⅓ cup (40g) chopped walnuts
¼ cup (15g) shredded coconut

DATE FILLING

1½ cups (250g) seeded dates, chopped coarsely
½ cup (110g) caster sugar
⅔ cup (160ml) water
⅓ cup (80ml) lemon juice

coffee and walnut cake

PREPARATION TIME   **COOKING TIME**

30g butter

1 tablespoon brown sugar

2 teaspoons ground cinnamon

200g walnuts, toasted

½ cup (125ml) milk

1 tablespoon dry instant coffee

185g butter, extra

1⅓ cups (300g) caster sugar

3 eggs

1 cup (150g) self-raising flour

¾ cup (110g) plain flour

TOFFEE

½ cup (110g) caster sugar

2 tablespoons water

3 teaspoons cream

1 Preheat oven to moderately slow. Thoroughly grease and lightly flour 22cm-baba cake pan; shake out excess flour.

2 Melt butter in small saucepan, add brown sugar, cinnamon and walnuts; stir well. Cool.

3 Combine milk and coffee in small bowl; stir until coffee dissolved.

4 Beat extra butter and caster sugar in small bowl with electric mixer until light and fluffy. Beat in eggs one at a time, beating until just combined between additions. Fold in sifted flours, then milk mixture.

5 Spread one third of the cake mixture in base of prepared pan, sprinkle with half walnut mixture, top with remaining cake mixture. Bake in moderately slow oven about 45 minutes or until cooked when tested. Stand cake 5 minutes before turning onto wire rack to cool.

6 Make toffee.

7 Place cake on wire rack over oven tray. Drizzle some of the toffee on top of cake, press on remaining walnut mixture; drizzle with remaining toffee.

   TOFFEE Combine sugar and the water in small saucepan. Stir over low heat until sugar dissolves. Bring to a boil, simmer, uncovered, until sugar browns slightly. Add cream and stir 1 minute or until thickened slightly.

serves 8

per serving 42.2g fat; 2996kJ (716 cal)

TIP Recipe is best made on the day of serving.

cherry friands

PREPARATION TIME   **COOKING TIME**

Friands can be made with a variety of fruits or nuts, but cherry friands are our favourite.

1½ cups (240g) icing sugar mixture
½ cup (75g) plain flour
185g butter, melted
6 egg whites, beaten lightly
1 cup (125g) almond meal
250g fresh cherries, halved, pitted

1 Preheat oven to moderately hot. Grease 12 small rectangular or oval friand pans or a 12-hole ⅓-cup (80ml) muffin pan.
2 Sift sugar and flour into medium bowl. Add butter, egg whites and almond meal; using wooden spoon, stir until just combined.
3 Divide mixture among prepared pans; top with cherries. Bake in moderately hot oven about 25 minutes. Stand 5 minutes; turn onto wire rack to cool. Serve warm or at room temperature.

makes 12
per friand 18.5g fat; 1209kJ (289 cal)
TIPS Cherries can be frozen for up to 18 months. Freeze them, in 250g batches, when they are in season. If you use frozen cherries, be sure to use them unthawed – this will minimise the "bleeding" of colour into the mixture. You can make an assortment of flavoured friands by using blueberries, bananas, strawberries or raspberries.

passionfruit butter biscuits

PREPARATION TIME   **COOKING TIME**

1 Combine butter, sugar and flours in large bowl of food processor;
   process 2 minutes or until mixture is combined. Add passionfruit;
   process until mixture clings together.
2 Transfer mixture to lightly floured surface; knead gently until smooth.
   Cut mixture in half, roll each half into 26cm log, wrap in plastic wrap;
   refrigerate 1 hour.
3 Preheat oven to moderately slow.
4 Cut logs into 1cm slices. Place slices about 3cm apart on lightly
   greased oven trays. Bake about 20 minutes or until pale golden
   colour. Cool on wire rack.

250g butter, softened
1⅓ cups (220g) icing sugar mixture
2 cups (300g) plain flour
½ cup (75g) cornflour
⅓ cup (50g) rice flour
2 tablespoons passionfruit pulp

makes 40
per biscuit 5.3g fat; 440kJ (105 cal)
TIP Recipe can be made a week ahead; store in an airtight container.

best-ever boiled fruit cake

PREPARATION TIME   **COOKING TIME**

2¼ cups (375g) sultanas

2 cups (340g) coarsely
   chopped raisins

1½ cups (225g) currants

½ cup (85g) mixed peel

¾ cup (150g) halved
   red glacé cherries

250g butter, chopped

1 cup (220g) firmly packed
   brown sugar

½ cup (125ml) brandy

½ cup (125ml) water

5 eggs, beaten lightly

2 tablespoons apricot jam

2 teaspoons finely grated
   orange rind

1 teaspoon finely grated
   lemon rind

1¾ cups (260g) plain flour

⅓ cup (50g) self-raising flour

½ teaspoon bicarbonate of soda

½ cup (80g) blanched almonds,
   for decoration

¼ cup (60ml) brandy, extra

1 Combine fruit, butter, sugar, brandy and the water in large saucepan. Stir constantly over heat, without boiling, until sugar is dissolved. Bring to a boil; reduce heat, simmer, covered, 10 minutes. Transfer mixture to large bowl; cool to room temperature.

2 Preheat oven to slow. Grease deep 19cm-square cake pan or a deep 22cm-round cake pan; line base and sides with two layers of brown paper and two layers of baking paper, bringing paper 5cm above edge of pan.

3 Add egg, jam and rinds to fruit mixture; stir until combined. Stir in sifted dry ingredients. Spread mixture evenly into prepared pan; arrange almonds on top. Bake in slow oven about 2½ to 3 hours. (Cover cake loosely with foil during cooking if it is over-browning).

4 Brush extra brandy over top of hot cake; cover tightly with foil, cool cake in pan.

serves 20
per serving 13.8g fat; 1742kJ (416 cal)

TIP This cake can be made up to three months ahead. Store in an airtight container in a cool, dry place, or refrigerate if the weather is humid.

chocolate ganache and raspberry cake

PREPARATION TIME   **COOKING TIME**

⅓ cup (35g) cocoa powder
⅓ cup (60ml) water
150g dark eating chocolate, melted
150g butter, melted
1⅓ cups (300g) firmly packed
    brown sugar
1 cup (125g) almond meal
4 eggs, separated
200g dark eating chocolate,
    chopped coarsely
⅔ cup (160ml) thickened cream
300g raspberries

1   Preheat oven to moderately slow. Grease deep 22cm-round cake pan;
    line base and side with baking paper.
2   Blend sifted cocoa powder with the water in large bowl until smooth.
    Stir in melted chocolate, butter, sugar, almond meal and egg yolks.
3   Beat egg whites in small bowl with electric mixer until soft peaks form;
    fold egg whites, in two batches, into chocolate mixture.
4   Pour mixture into prepared pan; bake, uncovered, in moderately slow
    oven about 1¼ hours. Stand cake 15 minutes then turn onto wire rack;
    turn cake top-side up to cool.
5   Stir chopped chocolate and cream in small saucepan over low heat
    until smooth.
6   Place raspberries on top of cake; drizzle chocolate mixture over
    raspberries. Stand cake at room temperature until chocolate sets.

serves 12
per serving 31.4g fat; 2019kJ (482 cal)
TIPS Undecorated cake is suitable to freeze.
The cake can be made up to three days in advance. Top cake
with raspberries and chocolate on the day of serving.
Chocolate and butter can be combined and melted in a saucepan
over low heat or in a microwave oven. Chopped chocolate and cream
can be heated together in a microwave oven.

upside-down chocolate caramel nut cake

PREPARATION TIME   **COOKING TIME**

2 tablespoons chopped unsalted
roasted macadamias

2 tablespoons chopped unsalted
roasted pistachios

2 tablespoons chopped unsalted
roasted walnuts

125g butter, chopped

1 cup (200g) firmly packed
brown sugar

3 eggs

1 cup (150g) self-raising flour

¼ cup (35g) plain flour

¼ teaspoon bicarbonate of soda

⅓ cup (35g) cocoa powder

100g dark eating chocolate, melted

¾ cup (180ml) milk

CARAMEL TOPPING

40g butter

¼ cup (55g) brown sugar

2 tablespoons cream

1 Preheat oven to moderately slow. Grease deep 20cm-round cake pan;
   line base with baking paper.

2 Make caramel topping.

3 Pour topping over base of prepared pan, sprinkle combined nuts over
   caramel; freeze while preparing cake mixture.

4 Beat butter and sugar in small bowl with electric mixer until light and
   fluffy. Beat in eggs one at a time, beating until just combined between
   each addition.

5 Stir in sifted flours, bicarbonate of soda and cocoa powder, then
   chocolate and milk.

6 Spread cake mixture over caramel topping. Bake in moderately slow
   oven about 1 hour 10 minutes. Stand cake 15 minutes before turning
   onto a wire rack to cool.

   CARAMEL TOPPING Combine butter, sugar and cream in small
   saucepan; stir over low heat, without boiling, until sugar is dissolved.
   Bring to a boil, then remove from heat.

serves 10

per serving 23.9g fat; 1742kJ (416 cal)

TIP Recipe can be made a day ahead.

rhubarb coconut cake

PREPARATION TIME   **COOKING TIME**

1½ cups (225g) self-raising flour
1¼ cups (275g) caster sugar
1¼ cups (110g) desiccated coconut
125g butter, melted
3 eggs, beaten lightly
½ cup (125ml) milk
1 teaspoon vanilla essence
¾ cup (90g) finely chopped rhubarb
2 stalks rhubarb (125g), extra
2 tablespoons demerara sugar

1 Preheat oven to moderate. Grease deep 20cm-round cake pan; line base with baking paper.
2 Combine flour, caster sugar and coconut in medium bowl; stir in butter, egg, milk and essence until combined.
3 Spread half the cake mixture into prepared pan; scatter chopped rhubarb evenly over cake mixture. Spread remaining batter over rhubarb.
4 Cut extra rhubarb into 5cm lengths. Arrange rhubarb pieces over top of cake, sprinkle with demerara sugar.
5 Bake in moderate oven about 1 hour 15 minutes. Stand cake 5 minutes before turning onto wire rack to cool.

serves 10
per serving 19.9g fat; 1626kJ (388 cal)
TIP Recipe can be made two days ahead.

hazelnut caramel slice

PREPARATION TIME 25 MINUTES **COOKING TIME** 35 MINUTES (PLUS COOLING AND REFRIGERATION TIME)

200g butter, chopped
½ cup (50g) cocoa powder
2 cups (440g) firmly packed
   brown sugar
1 teaspoon vanilla essence
2 eggs, beaten lightly
1½ cups (225g) plain flour
200g dark eating chocolate,
   melted, cooled
1 tablespoon vegetable oil

CARAMEL FILLING

180g butter, chopped
½ cup (110g) caster sugar
2 tablespoons golden syrup
¾ cup (180ml) sweetened
   condensed milk
1¼ cups (185g) whole hazelnuts,
   toasted

1 Preheat oven to moderately slow. Grease 20cm x 30cm lamington pan; line base and two sides with baking paper.

2 Combine butter and cocoa powder in medium saucepan, stir over low heat until smooth. Add sugar, stir until dissolved.

3 Remove from heat, add essence, egg and sifted flour; mix well. Spread mixture into prepared pan, bake in moderately slow oven 20 minutes; cool.

4 Meanwhile, make caramel filling. Quickly spread caramel filling evenly over base; refrigerate for at least 30 minutes or until firm.

5 Combine chocolate and oil in small bowl, spread over caramel filling; refrigerate until set, cut into pieces.

CARAMEL FILLING Combine butter, sugar, syrup and condensed milk in medium saucepan; stir over low heat until butter is melted. Increase heat to medium and simmer, stirring, about 13 minutes or until mixture is a dark caramel colour. Remove from heat, stir in hazelnuts.

makes 30
per slice 18g fat; 1257kJ (300 cal)
TIP Recipe can be made two days ahead; store in an airtight container in refrigerator.

shortbread crescents

PREPARATION TIME   **COOKING TIME**

250g butter, softened

⅓ cup (55g) icing sugar mixture

1 egg yolk

1 tablespoon brandy

½ cup (60g) almond meal

2 tablespoons chopped
  slivered almonds

2 cups (300g) plain flour

½ cup (75g) self-raising flour

1½ cups (240g) icing sugar
  mixture, extra

1   Preheat oven to moderate.

2   Beat butter and sugar in medium bowl with electric mixer until light and fluffy. Add egg yolk and brandy, beat until well combined. Stir in both almonds and sifted flours to form a soft dough (it may be easiest to do this using a low setting on an electric mixer).

3   Shape level tablespoons of mixture into crescents; place 3cm apart on ungreased baking trays. Bake crescents in moderate oven about 15 minutes or until browned lightly.

4   Cool shortbread on tray for 10 minutes. Sift half the extra sugar over a sheet of baking paper. Transfer shortbread onto icing sugar. Sift over the remaining sugar to coat completely.

makes 36

per crescent 7.2g fat; 564kJ (135 cal)

TIP   Recipe can be made a week ahead; store in an airtight container.

hazelnut and chocolate biscuits

PREPARATION TIME   **COOKING TIME**

1 Beat butter and sugars in small bowl with electric mixer until pale and fluffy. Stir in sifted flours in two batches; stir in milk and nuts.
2 Divide mixture in half. Knead each half until smooth; roll each half into 30cm log. Wrap logs in plastic wrap, refrigerate 1 hour or until firm.
3 Preheat oven to slow.
4 Cut logs into 8mm slices, place 3cm apart on greased oven trays. Bake about 20 minutes or until pale golden. Cool on wire rack.
5 Meanwhile, make hazelnut spread.
6 Join biscuits with a teaspoon of hazelnut spread. Serve dusted with icing sugar, if desired.
   HAZELNUT SPREAD Combine spread and chocolate in a bowl; refrigerate, stirring often, until spreadable.

makes 18
per biscuit 5.1g fat; 376kJ (90 cal)
TIP Biscuits can be made several days ahead. Join biscuits on day of serving.

60g butter
2 tablespoons caster sugar
2 tablespoons brown sugar
½ cup (75g) plain flour
1½ tablespoons rice flour
1 tablespoon cornflour
1 tablespoon milk
1½ tablespoons finely chopped toasted hazelnuts

HAZELNUT SPREAD
¼ cup (75g) chocolate hazelnut spread
30g dark cooking chocolate, melted

231

mud cake with satin chocolate glaze

PREPARATION TIME   **COOKING TIME**

250g butter, chopped

200g dark eating chocolate,
  chopped

2 cups (440g) caster sugar

1⅓ cups (330ml) water

1 tablespoon dry instant coffee

¾ cup (110g) plain flour

¾ cup (110g) self-raising flour

¼ cup (25g) cocoa powder

3 eggs, beaten lightly

silver cachous or dragée cake
  decorations (optional)

SATIN CHOCOLATE GLAZE

200g dark eating chocolate,
  chopped

⅔ cup (160ml) thickened cream

1 Grease deep 19cm-square cake pan; line base and sides with
  baking paper.

2 Combine butter, chocolate, sugar, the water and coffee in medium
  saucepan; stir over low heat, without boiling, until butter is just melted
  and mixture is smooth. Transfer chocolate mixture to large bowl, allow
  to cool for 10 minutes.

3 Preheat oven to slow.

4 Whisk combined sifted flours and cocoa powder into chocolate mixture
  in two batches, then whisk in eggs. Pour mixture into prepared pan.

5 Bake in slow oven about 1¾ hours. Cover cake pan with foil; cool
  cake in pan.

6 Make satin chocolate glaze.

7 Spread a thin layer of glaze all over cold cake. Stand remaining glaze
  at room temperature until thickened slightly, then spread over top and
  sides of cake. Sprinkle top with the decorations, if desired.

SATIN CHOCOLATE GLAZE   Combine chocolate and cream in medium
heatproof bowl; stir over barely simmering water until smooth.

serves 10
per serving 39.1g fat; 2961kJ (707 cal)

mixed berry buttermilk muffins

PREPARATION TIME 5 MINUTES **COOKING TIME** 20 MINUTES (PLUS STANDING TIME)

Muffins can be sweet or savoury and, although originally considered a breakfast bread, they are now eaten any time of the day. We used 50g frozen blueberries, 50g frozen blackberries and 100g frozen raspberries in this recipe.

2½ cups (375g) self-raising flour
¾ cup (165g) caster sugar
1 egg, beaten lightly
1 teaspoon vanilla essence
⅔ cup (160ml) vegetable oil
¾ cup (180ml) buttermilk
200g frozen mixed berries

1 Preheat oven to moderately hot. Line 12-hole ⅓-cup (80ml) muffin pan with paper cases or grease holes of pan.
2 Sift flour and sugar into large bowl; stir in remaining ingredients.
3 Divide mixture among muffin holes; bake in moderately hot oven about 20 minutes. Stand 5 minutes; turn onto wire rack, turn muffins top-side up to cool.

makes 12
per muffin 13.4g fat; 1192kJ (285 cal)
TIPS Be careful not to overmix muffin mixture; it should be slightly lumpy. Use still-frozen berries to minimise "bleeding" of colour into the mixture. These muffins freeze well; wrap them individually in plastic wrap so you only need to defrost a certain number of them at any time.

mini choc-chip friands

PREPARATION TIME   **COOKING TIME**

1 Preheat oven to moderate. Grease two 12-hole mini muffin pans.
2 Place egg whites in medium bowl; whisk lightly with fork until combined. Add butter, almond meal, sugar and flour to bowl; using wooden spoon, stir until just combined. Stir in chopped chocolate. Spoon tablespoons of mixture into pan holes.
3 Bake friands in moderate oven about 15 minutes or until browned lightly and cooked through. Turn onto wire racks to cool.
4 Combine cream and extra chocolate in medium heatproof bowl over pan of simmering water; stir until just melted. (Or, microwave on HIGH (100%) for about 1 minute. Stir mixture until smooth.) Stand until thickened. Spoon chocolate mixture over tops of friands.

3 egg whites
90g butter, melted
½ cup (60g) almond meal
¾ cup (120g) icing sugar mixture
¼ cup (35g) plain flour
100g dark eating chocolate, chopped finely
¼ cup (60ml) cream
100g dark eating chocolate, extra

makes 18
per friand 10.4g fat; 667kJ (159 cal)
TIP Recipe can be made a day ahead.

vanilla pear almond cake

PREPARATION TIME 30 MINUTES **COOKING TIME** 2 HOURS 15 MINUTES (PLUS COOLING AND STANDING TIME)

Corella is a small pear with a pale flesh and mild flavour.

8 small corella pears (800g)
2½ cups (625ml) water
1 strip lemon rind
1¾ cups (385g) caster sugar
1 vanilla bean
125g butter, chopped
3 eggs
⅔ cup (160g) sour cream
⅔ cup (100g) plain flour
⅔ cup (100g) self-raising flour
¼ cup (40g) blanched almonds, toasted, chopped coarsely
40g dark eating chocolate, chopped coarsely
½ cup (60g) almond meal

1 Peel pears, leaving stems intact.
2 Combine the water, rind and 1 cup of the sugar in medium saucepan. Split vanilla bean in half lengthways; scrape seeds into saucepan, then place pod in saucepan. Stir over heat, without boiling, until sugar dissolves. Add pears; bring to a boil. Reduce heat; simmer, covered, about 30 minutes or until pears are just tender. Transfer pears to medium bowl; bring syrup to a boil. Boil, uncovered, until syrup reduces by half. Cool completely.
3 Preheat oven to moderately slow. Insert base of 23cm springform tin upside down in tin to give a flat base; grease tin.
4 Beat butter and remaining sugar in medium bowl with electric mixer until light and fluffy. Add eggs, one at a time, beating until just combined between additions. Add sour cream; beat until just combined. (Mixture may curdle at this stage but will come together later.) Stir in 2 tablespoons of the syrup, then flours, nuts, chocolate and almond meal.
5 Spread cake mixture into prepared tin; place pears upright around edge of tin, gently pushing to the bottom. Bake, uncovered, in moderately slow oven about 1 hour 35 minutes. Stand 10 minutes; remove from tin.
6 Serve cake warm, brushed with remaining syrup.

serves 8
per serving 31.7g fat; 2628kJ (628 cal)

fudgy-wudgy chocolate cookies

PREPARATION TIME 15 MINUTES **COOKING TIME** 10 MINUTES (PLUS STANDING TIME)

125g butter, chopped

1 teaspoon vanilla essence

1¼ cups (275g) firmly packed
brown sugar

1 egg

1 cup (150g) plain flour

¼ cup (35g) self-raising flour

1 teaspoon bicarbonate of soda

⅓ cup (35g) cocoa powder

½ cup (85g) raisins

¾ cup (100g) macadamia nuts,
toasted, chopped coarsely

½ cup (95g) dark Choc Bits

½ cup (75g) dark chocolate
Melts, halved

1 Preheat oven to moderate. Line three oven trays with baking paper.
2 Beat butter, essence, sugar and egg in medium bowl with electric mixer until smooth. Stir in combined sifted flours, soda and cocoa powder; stir in raisins, nuts and both chocolates.
3 Drop rounded tablespoons of mixture onto prepared trays about 4cm apart; press each with fork to flatten slightly. Bake in moderate oven 10 minutes. Stand 5 minutes; transfer cookies to wire rack to cool.

makes 24
per cookie 10g fat; 802kJ (191 cal)
TIPS Cookies can be made up to one week ahead; store in an airtight container.
Other nuts, such as walnuts or pecans, can be used instead of macadamias.

moist whole orange cake

PREPARATION TIME **COOKING TIME**

1 Place unpeeled oranges in medium saucepan, cover with cold water. Bring to a boil. Boil, covered, 30 minutes; drain. Repeat process with fresh water, boil for 1 hour or until oranges are tender; drain, cool.

2 Grease and flour the side of deep 22cm-round cake pan; grease and line base with baking paper.

3 Process toasted blanched almonds with 2 tablespoons of the sugar until finely chopped.

4 Trim ends off oranges and discard. Halve oranges; remove and discard seeds. Process oranges, including rind, with baking powder until mixture becomes pulpy.

5 Preheat oven to moderate.

6 Beat eggs and remaining sugar in medium bowl about 3 minutes with electric mixer until fluffy and pale. Fold in almond mixture, almond meal, flour and then the orange pulp.

7 Pour mixture into prepared pan; bake in moderate oven about 1 hour or until cooked when tested. Cool in pan.

8 Turn cake onto serving plate and dust with icing sugar, if desired.

2 medium oranges (480g)
⅔ cup (110g) blanched almonds, toasted
1 cup (220g) caster sugar
1 teaspoon baking powder
6 eggs
2 cups (250g) almond meal
2 tablespoons plain flour

serves 10

per serving 22.5g fat; 1479kJ (353 cal)

TIP Recipe can be made two days ahead; store in an airtight container.

glossary

almonds flat, pointy-ended nuts with pitted brown shell enclosing a creamy white kernel, which is covered by a brown skin.

blanched: brown skins removed.

meal: also known as ground almonds. Nuts are powdered to a coarse flour texture; for use in baking or as a thickening agent.

slivered: small pieces cut lengthways.

vienna: toffee-coated almonds.

American-style pork spare ribs well-trimmed mid-loin ribs.

bacon rashers also known as bacon slices; made from cured and smoked pork side.

basil an aromatic herb; there are many types, but the most commonly used is sweet basil.

thai: also known as horapa. Is different from holy basil and sweet basil in both look and taste; it has smaller leaves and purplish stems, and a slight licorice or aniseed taste. It is one of the basic flavours that typify Thai cuisine.

bay leaves aromatic leaves from the bay tree used to flavour soups, stocks and casseroles.

beans, green sometimes called french or string beans (although the tough string they once had has generally been bred out), this long fresh bean is consumed pod and all.

bean sprouts also known as bean shoots; tender new growths of assorted beans and seeds germinated for consumption as sprouts. Most often used in stir-fries and salads. The most readily available are mung bean, soy bean, alfalfa and snow pea sprouts.

bean thread noodles also known as wun sen; made from extruded mung bean paste. Often known as cellophane or glass noodles because they are transparent when cooked. White in colour (not off-white like rice vermicelli), very delicate and fine; available dried in various size bundles.

beetroot also known as red beets; firm, round root vegetable.

bicarbonate of soda also known as baking soda.

black bean sauce a Chinese sauce made from fermented soy beans, spices, water and wheat flour, and is often used in stir-fry cooking.

blue swimmer crab also known as sand crab or atlantic blue crab.

bok choy also known as bak choy, pak choi, chinese white cabbage or chinese chard. Has a fresh, mild mustard taste; use stems and leaves.

baby bok choy: also known as pak kat farang, shanghai bok choy, chinese chard or white cabbage. Is smaller and more tender than bok choy. Use stems and leaves.

borlotti beans, canned also known as roman beans; can be eaten fresh or dried.

breadcrumbs, stale one- or two-day-old bread made into crumbs by grating, blending or processing.

butter use salted or unsalted (sweet) butter; 125g is equal to 1 stick butter.

buttermilk sold in the refrigerated dairy compartments in supermarkets. Originally just the liquid left after cream was separated from milk, today it is commercially made similarly to yogurt.

cabbage, savoy large, heavy head with crinkled dark-green outer leaves; a fairly mild-tasting cabbage.

cajun seasoning used to give an authentic US Deep South spicy cajun flavour to food. This packaged blend of assorted herbs and spices can include paprika, basil, onion, fennel, thyme, cayenne and tarragon.

calamari a type of squid.

capers the grey-green buds of a warm climate (usually Mediterranean) shrub; sold either dried and salted or pickled in a vinegar brine. Baby capers also are available.

capsicum also known as bell pepper or, simply, pepper. Native to Central and South America; can be red, green, yellow, orange or purplish black. Seeds and membranes should be discarded before use.

cheese

bocconcini: the term used for walnut-sized baby mozzarella; a delicate, semi-soft, white cheese traditionally made in Italy from buffalo milk. Spoils rapidly so must be kept under refrigeration, in brine, for 1 or 2 days at most.

cheddar: the most common cows milk 'tasty' cheese; should be aged, hard and have a pronounced bite.

cream cheese: also known as Philadelphia or Philly; a soft cows-milk cheese with a fat content of at least 33%. Sold at supermarkets in bulk and packaged.

fetta: Greek in origin; a crumbly textured goats- or sheep-milk cheese with a sharp, salty taste.

fontina: a smooth, firm cheese with a nutty taste and a brown or red rind.

goats: made from goats milk; has an earthy, strong taste. Available in both soft and firm textures, in various shapes and sizes; sometimes rolled in ash or herbs.

gorgonzola: a creamy Italian blue cheese having a mild, sweet taste; good as an accompaniment to fruit or to flavour sauces.

mascarpone: a cultured cream product made in much the same way as yogurt. It's whitish to creamy yellow in colour, with a soft, creamy texture.

parmesan: also known as parmigiano; is a hard, grainy, cows-milk cheese. The curd is salted in brine for a month before being aged for up to two years in humid conditions. Parmesan is mainly grated as a topping for pasta, soups and other savoury dishes, but is also delicious eaten with fruit.

pecorino: the generic Italian name for cheeses made from sheep milk. It's a hard, white to pale yellow cheese. Pecorino is usually matured for eight to 12 months. If unavailable, use parmesan.

ricotta: soft white cows-milk cheese; roughly translates as 'cooked again'. It's made from whey, a by-product of other cheese making, to which fresh milk and acid are added. It is a sweet, moist cheese, with a fat content of around 8.5% and a slightly grainy texture.

chicken breast fillets breasts halved, skinned and boned.

chicken tenderloins thin strip of meat lying just under the breast.

chilli available in many different types and sizes. Use rubber gloves when seeding and chopping fresh chillies as they can burn your skin. Removing seeds and membranes lessens the heat level.

banana: a sweet-flavoured chilli with a long, tapering shape. If unavailable, substitute with red capsicum.

dried flakes: deep-red, dehydrated, extremely fine slices and whole seeds; good for cooking or for sprinkling over cooked food in the same way as salt and pepper.

powder: the Asian variety is the hottest, made from dried ground thai chillies; it can be used as a substitute for fresh chillies in the proportion of ½ teaspoon ground chilli powder to 1 medium chopped fresh chilli.

sweet chilli sauce: the comparatively mild, thin thai sauce made from red chillies, sugar, garlic and vinegar; often used as a condiment.

thai red: small, medium hot and bright red in colour.

chinese broccoli also known as gai larn, kanah, gai lum, and chinese kale; appreciated more for its stems than its coarse leaves. Can be served steamed and stir-fried, in soups and noodle dishes.

chinese cabbage also known as peking or napa cabbage, wong bok or petsai. Elongated in shape with pale green, crinkly leaves; is the most common cabbage in South-East Asia. Can be shredded or chopped, and eaten raw or braised, steamed or stir-fried.

chives related to the onion and leek; has a subtle onion flavour. Garlic chives, also known as chinese chives, are strongly flavoured, have flat leaves and are eaten as a vegetable, usually in stir-fries.

chocolate hazelnut spread also known as Nutella.

chocolate

Choc Bits: are also known as chocolate chips and chocolate morsels; available in milk, white and dark chocolate. Made of cocoa liquor, cocoa butter, sugar and an emulsifier; hold their shape in baking and are ideal for decorating.

dark eating: made of cocoa liquor, cocoa butter and sugar.

Melts: are discs of compounded chocolate; ideal for melting and moulding.

white: eating chocolate.

ciabatta in Italian, the word means 'slipper', which is the traditional shape of this popular crisp-crusted white bread.

cocoa powder also known as cocoa; unsweetened cocoa beans that have been dried, roasted then finely ground.

coconut

desiccated: unsweetened, concentrated, dried, finely shredded coconut.

flaked: dried, flaked coconut flesh.

milk: diluted liquid from the second pressing of the white meat of a mature coconut (the first pressing produces coconut cream).

shredded: thin strips of dried coconut.

consommé clarified meat or fish stock.

corella pears miniature dessert pear up to 10cm long.

coriander also known as pak chee, cilantro or chinese parsley; bright-green-leafed herb with a pungent flavour. Often stirred into or sprinkled over a dish just before serving for maximum impact. Both the stems and roots of coriander also are used in Thai cooking; wash well before chopping.

cornflour also known as cornstarch; used as a thickening agent in cooking.

Craisins dried cranberries; are sold in most supermarkets.

cream, thickened (minimum fat content 35%) whipping cream containing a thickener.

crème de cacao a chocolate-flavoured liqueur. There are two different variations, dark and white. If a recipe calls for just crème de cacao, use the white (colourless) variety.

crème fraîche a naturally fermented cream (minimum fat content 35%) having a velvety texture and tangy taste.

cucumber, lebanese short, slender and thin-skinned; this variety is also known as the european or burpless cucumber.

cumin also known as zeera.

currants dried, tiny, almost black, raisins.

dates are green when unripe and turn yellow, golden brown, black or mahogany red — depending on the variety — as they ripen. Available fresh or dried, pitted or unpitted. The skin is thin and papery, and the flesh is extremely sweet. Choose plump, soft dates with a shiny skin.

eggs some recipes in this book call for raw or barely cooked eggs; exercise caution if there is a salmonella problem in your area.

egg noodles also known as ba mee or yellow noodles; made from wheat flour and eggs, and sold fresh or dried. Range in size from very fine strands to wide, thick spaghetti-like pieces as thick as a shoelace.

eggplant also known as aubergine. Ranging in size from tiny to very large, and in colour from pale green to deep purple; eggplant has an equally wide variety of flavours.

fennel also known as finocchio or anise. Also the name given to dried seeds having a licorice flavour.

fish sauce made from pulverised, salted, fermented fish (most often anchovies); has a pungent smell and a strong taste. There are many versions of varying intensity, so use according to your taste.

five-spice powder a fragrant mixture of ground cinnamon, cloves, star anise, sichuan pepper and fennel seeds.

flour

plain: an all-purpose flour, made from wheat.

rice: made from ground white rice.

self-raising: plain flour sifted with baking powder in the proportion of 1 cup flour to 2 teaspoons baking powder.

fruit mince also known as mince meat.

garam masala a blend of spices, originating in North India; consists of cardamom, cloves, cinnamon, coriander, fennel and cumin, roasted and ground together. Black pepper and chilli can be added for a hotter version.

gelatine we used powdered gelatine; also available in sheet form known as leaf gelatine.

ginger, fresh also known as green or root ginger; the thick root of a tropical plant.

glacé fruit fruit that is cooked in a heavy sugar syrup then dried.

golden syrup a by-product of refined sugarcane; pure maple syrup or honey can be substituted.

green curry paste the hottest of the traditional pastes. Particularly good in chicken and vegetable curries; a great addition to stir-fries and noodle dishes.

hazelnuts also known as filberts; plump, grape-size, rich, sweet nut having a brown inedible skin that is removed by rubbing heated nuts together in a tea towel.

hoisin sauce a thick, sweet and spicy chinese paste made from salted, fermented soy beans, onions and garlic; used as a marinade or baste, or to accent stir-fries and barbecued or roasted foods.

hokkien noodles also known as stir-fry noodles; fresh wheat noodles resembling thick, yellow-brown spaghetti, needing no pre-cooking before being used.

iceberg lettuce a heavy, firm, round lettuce with tightly packed leaves and crisp texture.

jam also known as preserve or conserve; most often made from fruit.

kaffir lime leaf also known as bai magrood; looks like two glossy dark green leaves joined end to end, forming a rounded hourglass shape. Used like bay leaves or curry leaves, especially in thai cooking. Available from Asian food stores and specialty greengrocers. Freeze any remaining leaves for future use.

kecap manis also known as ketjap manis; a thick soy sauce with added sugar and spices.

kumara Polynesian name of orange-fleshed sweet potato, often confused with yam.

lemon grass a tall, clumping, lemon-smelling and -tasting, sharp-edged grass; the white lower part of the stem is used, finely chopped, in cooking.

lentils dried pulses often identified by and named after their colour (red, brown, yellow).

lima beans large, flat, kidney-shaped, beige, dried and canned beans. Also known as butter beans.

mesclun a salad mix of assorted young lettuce and other green leaves, including baby spinach, mizuna and curly endive.

mince meat also known as ground meat, as in beef, pork, chicken, lamb and veal.

mint, vietnamese not a mint at all, but a pungent and peppery narrow-leafed member of the buckwheat family. It is a common ingredient in thai cooking, particularly soups, salads and stir-fries.

mint jelly a condiment usually served with roast lamb; packaged or homemade jelly flavoured with mint flakes.

mirin a Japanese champagne-coloured cooking wine made of glutinous rice and alcohol expressly for cooking, and should not be confused with sake. There is a seasoned sweet mirin called manjo mirin that is made of water, rice, corn syrup and alcohol.

mixed peel candied citrus peel.

mushroom

button: small, cultivated white mushrooms with a mild flavour.

cap: slightly larger and with a stronger flavour than buttons, caps, sometimes called cups, are firm textured and ideal for soups, pies and casseroles.

enoki: clumps of long, spaghetti-like stems with tiny, snowy-white caps.

flat: large, flat mushrooms with a rich, earthy flavour, ideal for filling and barbecuing. They are sometimes misnamed field mushrooms, which are wild mushrooms.

shiitake: also known as donko or chinese mushrooms; available fresh and dried.

swiss brown: light to dark brown mushrooms with full-bodied flavour, also known as roman or cremini. Button or cap mushrooms can be substituted.

mussels buy from a fish market where there is reliably fresh fish. Must be tightly closed when bought, indicating they are alive. Before cooking, scrub shells with a strong brush and remove the 'beards'. Discard any shells that do not open after cooking.

mustard

dijon: a pale brown, distinctively flavoured, fairly mild French mustard.

wholegrain: also known as seeded. A French-style coarse-grain mustard made from crushed mustard seeds and dijon-style French mustard.

oak leaf lettuce also known as Feuille de Chene. Available in both red and green leaf. Green oak leaf lettuce, also known as leaf lettuce, has soft, frilled leaves, a large heart and mild flavour.

oil

olive: made from ripened olives. Extra virgin and virgin are the first and second press, respectively, of the olives, while extra light or light is diluted and refers to taste, not fat levels.

peanut: pressed from ground peanuts; most commonly used oil in asian cooking because of its high smoke point (capacity to handle high heat without burning).

sesame: made from roasted, crushed, white sesame seeds; a flavouring rather than a cooking medium.

spray: we used a cholesterol-free cooking spray made from canola oil.

vegetable: any of a number of oils sourced from plants rather than animal fats.

onion

green: also known as scallion or, incorrectly, shallot; an immature onion picked before the bulb has formed, having a long, bright-green edible stalk.

red: also known as spanish, red spanish or bermuda onion; a sweet-flavoured, large, purple-red onion.

shallot: also called golden shallot or eschalot; small, elongated, brown-skinned member of the onion family. Grows in tight clusters similar to garlic.

oyster sauce Asian in origin; a rich, brown sauce made from oysters and their brine, cooked with salt and soy sauce, and then thickened with starches.

pancetta Italian bacon that is cured, but not smoked.

pappadums sun-dried wafers made from a combination of lentil and rice flours, oil and spices.

paprika ground, dried red capsicum (bell pepper), available sweet or hot.

parsley, flat-leaf also known as continental parsley or italian parsley.

pastry

ready rolled puff: packaged sheets of frozen puff pastry.

ready rolled shortcrust: packaged sheets of frozen shortcrust pastry.

pearl barley has had its outer husk (bran) removed, and has been steamed and polished before being used in cooking.

peri peri sauce portuguese chilli sauce. A blend of chilli, garlic, oil and spices. Available from specialty delicatessens.

pine nuts also known as pignoli; not, in fact, a nut, but a small, cream-coloured kernel from pine cones.

pitta bread also known as lebanese bread. A wheat-flour pocket bread sold in large, flat pieces that can be separated into two thin

rounds. Also available in small thick pieces called pocket pitta.

plum sauce a thick, sweet and sour dipping sauce made from plums, vinegar, sugar, chillies and spices.

polenta a flour-like cereal made of dried corn (maize), also known as cornmeal; sold ground in several different textures. Also the name of the dish made from it.

prawns also known as shrimp.

prosciutto cured, air-dried (unsmoked), pressed ham.

radicchio burgundy-leaved lettuce with white ribs and slightly bitter flavour.

raisins dried sweet grapes.

red curry paste probably the most popular curry paste; a hot blend of different flavours that complements the richness of pork, duck and seafood. Also works well in marinades and sauces.

rice noodles, fresh can be purchased in various widths or large sheets, which are cut into the noodle width desired. Chewy and pure white, they do not need pre-cooking before use.

rice paper wrappers made from rice paste and stamped into rounds; store well at room temperature. They are quite brittle, and will break if dropped; dipped momentarily in water they become pliable wrappers for fried food and uncooked vegetables. Make good spring-roll wrappers.

rice

arborio: small, round grain rice well-suited to absorb a large amount of liquid; especially suitable for risottos.

long-grain: elongated grain, remains separate when cooked; popular steaming rice in Asia.

rocket also known as arugula, rugula and rucola; a peppery-tasting green leaf that can be eaten raw in salad or used in cooking. Baby rocket leaves are both smaller and less peppery.

saffron threads available in strands or ground form; imparts a yellow-orange colour to food once infused. Quality varies greatly; the best is the most expensive spice in the world. Should be stored in the freezer.

scallops a bivalve mollusc with fluted shell valve; we use scallops having the coral (roe).

seasoned salt to make your own: combine 2 tablespoons coarse kitchen salt with ½ teaspoon five-spice powder in heavy-based pan. Stir over low heat for 2 minutes.

sesame seeds available as black, white, red or brown seeds. A good source of calcium; used in cuisines the world over either as an ingredient in cooking or as a condiment. To toast: spread seeds evenly on oven tray, toast in moderate oven briefly.

shrimp paste also known as kapi, trasi and blanchan; a strong-scented, very firm preserved paste made of salted dried shrimp. Used as a pungent flavouring in many South-East Asian soups and sauces. It should be chopped or sliced thinly then wrapped in foil and roasted before use.

snow peas also called mange tout ('eat all'). Snow pea tendrils, the growing shoots of the plant, are sold by green grocers.

sour cream, light we used light sour cream with 18.5% fat.

soy sauce also known as sieu, is made from fermented soy beans. Several variations are available in most supermarkets and Asian food stores. We used a mild Japanese variety.

speck smoked pork.

spinach also known as english spinach and, incorrectly, silverbeet. Tender green leaves are good uncooked in salads or added to soups, stir-fries and stews just before serving

sponge finger biscuits also known as savoiardi biscuits, Savoy biscuits or lady's fingers; they are Italian-style crisp fingers made from sponge-cake mixture.

spring roll wrappers also called egg-roll wrappers; they come in various sizes, and can be purchased, either fresh or frozen, from Asian supermarkets.

squid hood a type of mollusc; also known as calamari. Buy squid hoods to make preparation easier.

star anise a dried star-shaped pod whose seeds have an astringent aniseed flavour; used to favour stocks and marinades.

stock available in cans, tetra packs, cubes or powder. As a guide, 1 teaspoon of stock powder or 1 small crumbled stock cube or 1 portion stock concentrate mixed with 1 cup (250ml) water will give a fairly strong stock.

sugar we used coarse, granulated table sugar, also known as crystal sugar, unless otherwise specified.

brown: finely granulated sugar retaining molasses for its characteristic colour.

caster: also known as superfine or finely granulated table sugar.

demerara: small-grained golden-coloured crystal sugar.

icing sugar mixture: also known as confectioners' sugar or powdered sugar; pulverised granulated sugar crushed together with a small amount (about 3%) cornflour added.

palm: also known as nam tan pip, jaggery, jawa or gula melaka; made from the sap of the sugar palm tree. Light brown to black in colour and usually sold in rock-hard cakes; substitute it with brown sugar if unavailable.

sultanas dried, seedless white grapes.

sweetened condensed milk from which 60% of the water had been removed; the remaining milk is then sweetened with sugar.

tandoori paste consisting of garlic, ginger, tamarind, coriander, chilli and spices.

Toblerone bars made from sugar, milk powder, cocoa, honey, almonds, glucose and egg white.

tofu, firm (tao hu) also known as bean curd; an off-white, custard-like product made from the 'milk' of crushed soy beans. Comes fresh as soft or firm, and processed as fried or pressed dried sheets. Leftover fresh tofu can be refrigerated in water (which is changed daily) up to four days.

tomato

canned: whole peeled tomatoes in natural juices.

cherry: also known as Tiny Tim or Tom Thumb tomatoes; are small and round.

egg: also called Plum or Roma, these are smallish, oval-shaped tomatoes much used in italian cooking or salads.

grape: baby egg tomatoes.

paste: triple-concentrated tomato puree used to flavour soups, stews, sauces and casseroles.

semi-dried: partially dried tomato pieces in olive oil; softer and juicier than sun-dried, these are not a preserve, thus do not keep as long as sun-dried.

sun-dried: we used sun-dried tomatoes packaged in oil, unless otherwise specified.

teardrop: small yellow pear-shaped tomatoes.

truss: small vine-ripened tomatoes with vine still attached.

tortillas thin, round unleavened bread that originated in Mexico; can be purchased frozen, fresh or vacuum-packed or made at home. Two kinds are available, one made from wheat flour and the other from corn.

turmeric, ground also known as kamin. Is a rhizome related to galangal and ginger; must be grated or pounded to release its somewhat acrid aroma and pungent flavour. Known for the golden colour it imparts to the dishes of which it's a part. Fresh turmeric can be substituted with the more common dried powder (use 2 teaspoons of ground turmeric plus a teaspoon of sugar for every 20g of fresh turmeric called for in a recipe).

vanilla bean dried long, thin pod from a tropical golden orchid; the minuscule black seeds inside the bean are used to impart a luscious vanilla flavour in baking and desserts. A whole bean can be placed in the sugar container to make the vanilla sugar often called for in recipes.

essence: distilled from the seeds of the vanilla pod; imitation vanilla extract is not a satisfactory substitute.

vermicelli noodles also known as sen mee, mei fun or bee hoon. Similar to bean threads, only are longer and made with rice flour instead of mung bean starch.

vinegar

apple cider: made from fermented apples.

balsamic: authentic only from the province of Modena, Italy; made from a regional wine of white Trebbiano grapes, specially processed then aged in antique wooden casks to give the exquisite pungent flavour.

red wine: based on fermented red wine.

rice: a colourless vinegar made from fermented rice and flavoured with sugar and salt. Also known as seasoned rice vinegar. Sherry can be substituted.

witlof also known as chicory or belgian endive. Cigar-shaped, tightly packed heads with pale, yellow-green tips. Has a delicately bitter flavour. May be cooked or eaten raw.

wonton wrappers also known as wonton skins; made of flour, eggs and water, they come in varying thicknesses. Usually sold packaged in large amounts, and found in the refrigerated section of Asian grocery stores; gow gee, egg or spring-roll pastry sheets can be substituted.

worcestershire sauce a thin, dark-brown spicy sauce used as a seasoning for meat, gravies, cocktails and as a condiment.

yeast allow 2 teaspoons (7g) dried granulated yeast to each 15g fresh yeast.

yogurt we used unflavoured full-fat yogurt in our recipes.

zucchini also known as courgette; small green, yellow or white vegetable belonging to the squash family. The zucchini flower is also edible.

index

facts and figures

Wherever you live, you'll be able to use our recipes with the help of these easy-to-follow conversions. While these conversions are approximate only, the difference between an exact and the approximate conversion of various liquid and dry measures is but minimal and will not affect your cooking results.

dry measures

metric	imperial
15g	1/2oz
30g	1oz
60g	2oz
90g	3oz
125g	4oz (1/4lb)
155g	5oz
185g	6oz
220g	7oz
250g	8oz (1/2lb)
280g	9oz
315g	10oz
345g	11oz
375g	12oz (3/4lb)
410g	13oz
440g	14oz
470g	15oz
500g	16oz (1lb)
750g	24oz (1 1/2lb)
1kg	32oz (2lb)

liquid measures

metric	imperial
30ml	1 fluid oz
60ml	2 fluid oz
100ml	3 fluid oz
125ml	4 fluid oz
150ml	5 fluid oz (1/4 pint/1 gill)
190ml	6 fluid oz
250ml	8 fluid oz
300ml	10 fluid oz (1/2 pint)
500ml	16 fluid oz
600ml	20 fluid oz (1 pint)
1000ml (1 litre)	1 3/4 pints

helpful measures

metric	imperial
3mm	1/8in
6mm	1/4in
1cm	1/2in
2cm	3/4in
2.5cm	1in
5cm	2in
6cm	2 1/2in
8cm	3in
10cm	4in
13cm	5in
15cm	6in
18cm	7in
20cm	8in
23cm	9in
25cm	10in
28cm	11in
30cm	12in (1ft)

measuring equipment

The difference between one country's measuring cups and another's is, at most, within a 2 or 3 teaspoon variance. (For the record, one Australian metric measuring cup holds approximately 250ml.) The most accurate way of measuring dry ingredients is to weigh them. When measuring liquids, use a clear glass or plastic jug with the metric markings. (One Australian metric tablespoon holds 20ml; one Australian metric teaspoon holds 5ml.)

Note: North America, NZ and the UK use 15ml tablespoons. All cup and spoon measurements are level.

We use large eggs having an average weight of 60g.

how to measure

When using graduated metric measuring cups, shake dry ingredients loosely into the appropriate cup. Do not tap the cup on a bench or tightly pack the ingredients unless directed to do so. Level top of measuring cups and measuring spoons with a knife. When measuring liquids, place a clear glass or plastic jug with metric markings on a flat surface to check accuracy at eye level.

oven temperatures

These oven temperatures are only a guide. Always check the manufacturer's manual.

	°C (Celsius)	°F (Fahrenheit)	Gas Mark
Very slow	120	250	1/2
Slow	140 – 150	275 – 300	1 – 2
Moderately slow	170	325	3
Moderate	180 – 190	350 – 375	4 – 5
Moderately hot	200	400	6
Hot	220 – 230	425 – 450	7 – 8
Very hot	240	475	9

Senior Editor *Wendy Bryant*
Designer *Caryl Wiggins*
Food editor *Louise Patniotis*
Special feature photographer *Brett Stevens*
Special feature stylist *Opel Khan*
Special feature home economist *Elizabeth Macri*
Assistant home economist *Sharon Reeve*
Food director *Pamela Clark*
Nutritional information *Laila Ibram*

The Australian Women's Weekly
Food director *Lyndey Milan*
Food editor *Alexandra McCowan*
Deputy food editor *Frances Abdallaoui*

ACP Books
Editorial director *Susan Tomnay*
Creative director *Hieu Chi Nguyen*
Editorial coordinator *Caroline Lowry*
Editorial assistant *Karen Lai*
Publishing manager (sales) *Brian Cearnes*
Publishing manager (rights & new projects) *Jane Hazell*
Brand manager *Donna Gianniotis*
Pre-press *Harry Palmer*

Production manager *Carol Currie*
Business manager *Seymour Cohen*
Assistant business analyst *Martin Howes*
Chief executive officer *John Alexander*
Group publisher *Pat Ingram*
Publisher *Sue Wannan*
Editor-in-chief *Deborah Thomas*

Produced by ACP books, Sydney.
Printed by SNP Leefung, China.
Published by ACP Publishing Pty Limited, 54 Park St, Sydney;
GPO Box 4088, Sydney, NSW 1028. Ph: (02) 9282 8618 Fax: (02) 9267 9438.
www.acpbooks.com.au

To order books phone 136 116.
Send recipe enquiries to reccipeenquiries@acp.com.au
AUSTRALIA: Distributed by Network Services,GPO Box 4088, Sydney, NSW 1028.
Ph: (02) 9282 8777 Fax: (02) 9264 3278.
UNITED KINGDOM: Distributed by Australian Consolidated Press (UK),
Moulton Park Business Centre, Red House Rd, Moulton Park, Northampton, NN3 6AQ
Ph: (01604) 497 531 Fax: (01604) 497 533 acpukltd@aol.com
CANADA: Distributed by Whitecap Books Ltd, 351 Lynn Ave,
North Vancouver, BC, V7J 2C4
Ph: (604) 980 9852 Fax: (604) 980 8197
customerservice@whitecap.ca www.whitecap.ca
NEW ZEALAND: Distributed by Netlink Distribution Company,
Level 4, 23 Hargreaves St, College Hill, Auckland 1, Ph: (9) 302 7616.

Clark, Pamela
The Australian Women's Weekly Best Food Collection
Includes index.
ISBN 1 86396 366 9
1.Cookery. I. Title. II. Title: Australian Women's Weekly

641.5
© ACP Publishing Pty Limited 2004
ABN 18 053 273 546
This publication is copyright. No part of it may be reproduced or transmitted in
any form without the written permission of the publishers.

Cover: Tangy lemon tart, page 208
Photographer: Brett Stevens
Stylist: Amber Keller

Back cover
Photographer: Brett Stevens
Stylist: Opel Khan

Photographers: Alan Benson; Steve Brown; Ben Dearnley; Joe Filshie; Ian Hofstetter
Chris Jones; Louise Lister; Mark O'Meara; Tim Robinson; Brett Stevens

Stylists: Wendy Berecry; Julz Beresford; Kirsty Cassidy; Marie-Helene Clauzon;
Georgina Dolling; Carolyn Fienberg; Jane Hann; Mary Harris; Katy Holder;
Amber Keller; Cherise Koch; Suzie Smith; Sophia Young